Tales from Montana's Sun River Country
from Choteau to the Dearborn River

The remarkable people, weather, crimes and events that made the local weekly news.

Also by Nancy C. Thornton

Tales from
Montana's Rocky Mountain Front

Tales from Montana's Teton County

Tales from Choteau Montana

The Birch Creek Hangings
and other Montana Tales from Choteau to Glacier Park

Tales from Montana's Sun River Country
from Choteau to the Dearborn River

The remarkable people, weather, crimes and events that made the local weekly news.

Nancy C. Thornton

Canal Heritage Enterprises
Choteau, Montana
2023

Cover Design: Ralph Thornton.
Front Cover: The view south of the South Fork of the Sun River at Bear Creek in the Bob Marshall Wilderness, Montana, Copyright ©2013 Ralph Thornton. Inset photograph: Sun River below Gibson Dam, Copyright ©2006 Ralph Thornton.

Back Cover: The Sawtooth Ridge guards the entrance to the Sun River Canyon. Copyright ©2009 Ralph Thornton. Inset photograph of the author, Copyright ©2016 Nancy C. Thornton.

The stories for this volume were written by Nancy C. Thornton and were originally published in the Choteau Acantha weekly newspaper. This volume has minor edits in the text for clarity. Grateful acknowledgment is made to the Choteau Acantha for permission to use copyrighted material.

First Printing: 2023

ISBN 978-0-9700704-7-0

Canal Heritage Enterprises
P.O. Box 1482
Choteau MT 59422
www.canalheritage.com

Contents

Acknowledgements

I would like to thank the Choteau Acantha publishers, Jeff and Melody Martinsen, and my husband, Ralph Thornton, without whose help this book would never have been completed.

Preface

"Life is like a landscape. You live in the midst of it but can describe it only from the vantage point of distance." — *Charles Lindbergh*

My interest in local history was honed by spending more than 25 years living near the small community of Lemont, Illinois, in the Illinois and Michigan Canal National Heritage Corridor, a narrowly-defined geographic area with a rich history and a few century-old local newspapers that documented that history.

After moving to Choteau, Montana, with my husband, Ralph, in 1999, I became intrigued by that same intensely local focus that the Choteau Acantha newspaper brought to its readers. I became a subscriber to and an employee of the Acantha.

The Choteau Acantha's "local news" focus is and always has been a paramount goal of its succession of publishers and editors since 1894. And so, the merging of my interest in the local history of the Rocky Mountain Front, Teton County and its county seat of Choteau naturally developed after reading the old newspapers of the region. They memorialize the history of the communities along the Front as does no other resource. ▰

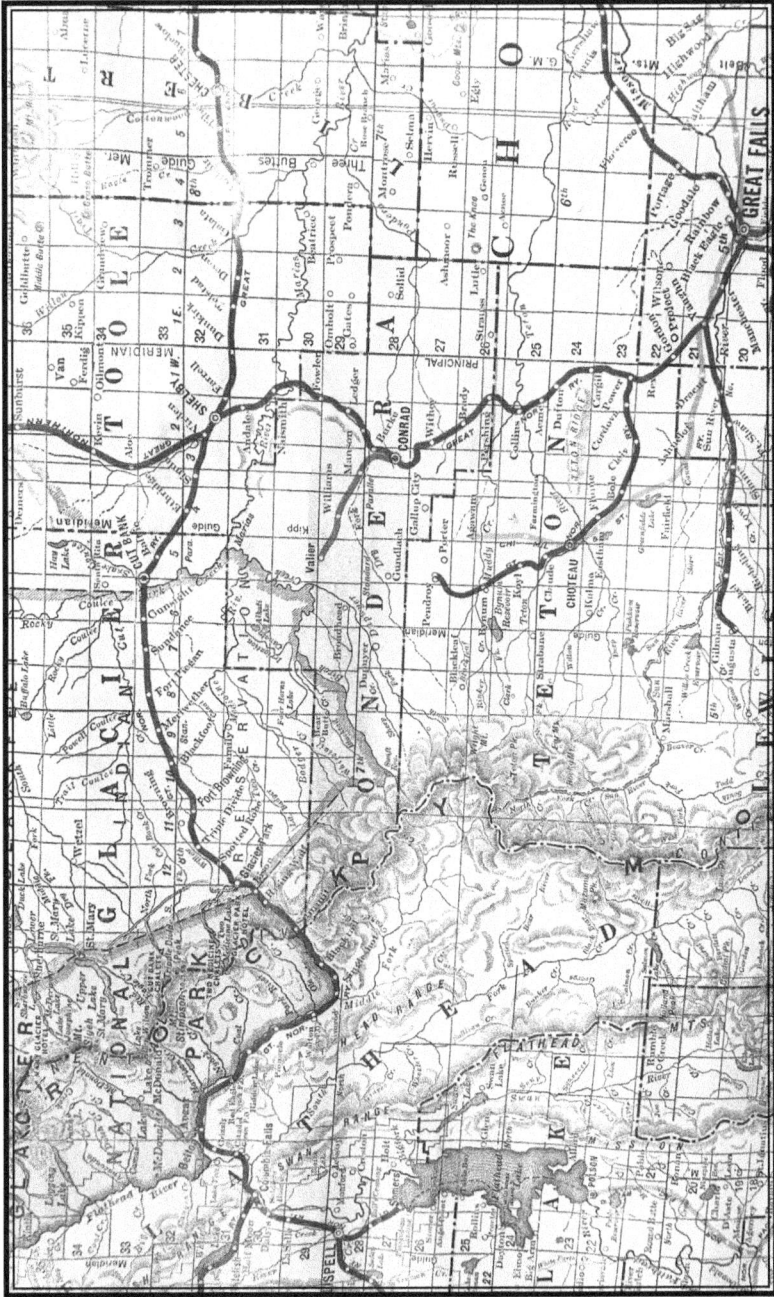

Map of the Great Northern Railway circa 1923. Source: Havre Railway Museum collection, 2018.

Introduction

The Sun River begins in the Rocky Mountains and ends at its junction with the Missouri River in Great Falls, Montana. It forms the southern boundary of Teton County, Montana, for a portion of its middle length. Its banks were some of the earliest territory settled by pioneers exploring north from Helena and west from Fort Benton.

According to author Roberta Carkeek Cheney, in her book, "Names on the Face of Montana," "An Indian name for the river, Natae-oueti, was translated by French trappers to mean 'medicine' or 'sun.'"

The tales that follow are mostly about the people, events and places in the southwestern region of northcentral Montana, including Choteau, Fairfield, Augusta and the Helena-Lewis and Clark National Forest southwest of Choteau. The stories are true, or as true as the newspaper editors of the past believed to be true. Here and there the editors of the day left out information deemed too sensitive for their readers and those details are now lost to history.

The oldest stories in this volume are gleaned from research in Helena, Fort Benton, Anaconda and Choteau newspapers. Starting about 1885, Choteau had its own newspaper. The news reports about Sun River, Fort Shaw, Fairfield, and the Dearborn River valley expanded as more of those communities started newspapers. At the time of the research for the stories about the Sun River country told here, those old newspapers were not available online. They have since been digitized.

This is the fifth book in a series, the first, "Tales from the Rocky Mountain Front," captures stories from the 1870s to 1935, including the birth of Choteau. The book, "Tales from Montana's Teton County," captures stories from the 1920s to the 2000s, and the "Tales from Choteau Montana," captures stories generated about and near the city of Choteau. The book, "The Birch Creek Hangings and other Montana Tales from Choteau to Glacier Park," captures stories about the region north of Choteau and Glacier National Park.

Readers have enjoyed these old news tales published in the weekly Choteau Acantha newspaper since 1999. This fifth volume introduces new readers to the local history of the region south of Choteau for the most part.

For readers who want to read the original newspaper pages, visit the Montana Historical Society's website, www.montananewspapers.org. To read the current Choteau Acantha, visit the website, www.choteauacantha.com.

This book presents a collection of previously published stories highlighting local history, in mostly chronological order based on the year generally taken from story's subject matter. Some text in this volume was edited or condensed from the original "It's old news" columns for clarity and to correct errors and conserve space as needed.

Packer and Guide James Hannon

1884-1919

The Rev. Leon F. Haley, a minister for the Episcopal church in Choteau in 1914, wrote about his adventures and the doings in town.

He traveled with a forest ranger to the Sun River country (in winter, no less) and documented the trip in the Choteau Montanan newspaper, the Choteau Acantha's competitor. The Acantha had a short mention on Jan. 7, "Claude 'Mud' Townsend's hurried trip to this city on the 3rd inst. was easily accounted for, when upon departing, he took with him one Rev. Haley, of knot-tying fame."

Townsend had been transferred to the Sun River district for the winter months, in place of his brother Price, who became acting forest supervisor. Mud and Haley first stopped at Mud's old post at the Ear Mountain Ranger Station to gather his things. They then traveled to the North Fork of the Sun River and to the Hannan Gulch Ranger Station.

Haley's account of his trip, published in three parts in January 1914, included this story. "Jim Hannan was a man of refined taste and good habits. He was a frontiersman with all that the name implies, and when he selected this gulch as a place to locate his cabin, he wooed splendid judgment. He had his friends as well as his enemies.

"His friends stood by him, and his enemies persecuted him. Bill Flowerre, [also spelled Flowerree and Floweree] one of the biggest cattlemen of this country, stood sponsor for his labors. When Hannan was in need of money, he called

upon Flowerre. He became a valuable man for Flowerre after he had established his residence in these mountains.

"Flowerre ran thousands of cattle up in Sun River Canyon. Beech, another member of the big cattle outfit, made
use of this range to a large extent, and when his men drove
out their stock in the fall, it was claimed by Flowerre that
Flowerre's cattle were included in the drive.

"It was Hannan's duty to take care of Flowerre's interest
against the depredations of Beech's men, and when Hannan
began to interfere, he was at once accused by Beech as being
a cattle rustler which in the ranch country is the next thing
to being a horse thief. Flowerre placed spies in the canyon
who kept a close eye on Jim, but they could not get anything on him. Finally, they put up a deal in the case of a big
steer, saying he had attempted to change the brand. Hannan had no witnesses to defend him, and he was obliged to
sell out his interests to his friend Chas. Jackson.

"This is the reason Jim Hannan left the country. It was
the case of the big fish eating the little ones. Hannan had
once killed a man in Augusta, and he had been wantonly
persecuted for this act. The victim was a Mexican [cowboy]
who entered a corral when Jim was saddling his horse. He
struck Jim several times with a heavy stock, and from all
appearances, it was his intent and purpose to slay him. In
self defense Jim shot at him with the idea of frightening
him away, but in the fray the [cowboy] was shot and died
shortly afterwards. Hannan was discharged in both the justice and the district courts, and there is no doubt that he
regretted the affair as much as did that of his friends.

"This is the history of Jim Hannan, and his cattle rus-
tling. He had his faults and committed his sins like the rest,
but he was no doubt a victim of unfortunate circumstances. His cabin is neatly built and shows all the earmarks of
a careful workman. The Forest Service has taken over the

property, and is making good use of the hay meadows and buildings. I have seen many mountain homes both in the Rockies and the Adirondacks back home, but I have never lived in a more home-like cabin where the sun seemed to shine more friendly than here in Hannan Gulch. Price Townsend has put in a big grubstake and makes this his home when on his forest duties. I admire his choice and appreciate his hospitality."

Haley told the tale and the old newspapers fill in some colorful details to corroborate the story.

Firstly, James P. Hannon was the man's real name, but by the early 20th century the spelling became Hannan Gulch. Hannon came to the Sun River Canyon/Augusta area in 1884. In December 1887 he filed a notice of final entry for a quarter section of land located about two and a half miles east of the present U.S. Forest Service boundary between Benchmark and Smith Creek roads west of Augusta.

There's no indication he got a land patent for that tract, because by 1894 he had established a cabin in a beautiful gulch about 25 miles up the North Fork of the Sun River. He worked as a cattle ranch hand and as a packer and guide.

But first he became known for killing a man on July 5, 1898. Statewide papers covered the story, as well as the local Choteau papers, the latter showing a favorable bias for the longtime resident of the area.

The Great Falls Tribune's story on July 6, read: "Homicide at Augusta. July 5 — Early this morning William Noel was shot three times and instantly killed by the last shot by James Hannon. The last shot passed through the heart.

"The two men were in the rear of Nett and Parker's livery stable. Both had been drinking and were quarreling. Noel seized a quirt and struck Hannon with it several times, whereupon the latter seized a 30-caliber rifle and shot his assailant.

"Noel was not well known here, but Hannon has been a resident of this section for many years. He has been employed on several ranches in this vicinity and of late has been engaged in the cattle business on the North Fork of the Sun River.

"Hannon is between 40 and 45 years of age and is said to be always peaceable and has a good reputation. Noel is about 35 years old. Noel was employed as cowboy on the Floweree ranch north of Augusta. Hannon is well known by many in Great Falls by reason of his having been a guide for nearly all parties who have visited the springs up Sun River. He has run a pack train and piloted many visitors to that section."

The Anaconda Standard embellished a few details, and so the real story may never be known. "Great Falls, July 5. Murders seem to be getting of common occurrence in Northern Montana. Tonight the little town of Augusta is all stirred up over the fatal conclusion of a feud there which has been of long standing. It is difficult to obtain the story tonight, there are so many conflicting reports and rumors afloat in the town, and they seem irreconcilable. The inquest will be held this evening, however, and will probably decide which is the true version.

"So far as can be learned these facts are admitted: William Nole [sic] and James Hannon have been on bad terms for a long time. Hannon had a horse in the livery stable at Augusta and this morning at 12:45, that is, shortly after midnight, he went into the stable to find how his horse was getting along.

"He passed through the stable to the corral in the rear where he met Nole. They had some words and then Nole struck Hannon with a loaded quirt. Hannon tried to get away, but Nole kept striking him, until Hannon finally drew a revolver and fired three shots. It is not known which of the shots took effect or whether all of them were not fatal. Hannon surrendered himself to Constable Zimmer, who still has him in charge."

Hannon claimed self defense. The coroner's jury at the inquest returned a verdict that deceased came to his death through "justifiable defense" as they put it. "The county attorney does not like the verdict, and accordingly swore out a warrant for Hannon's arrest, charging him with murder in the first degree," the newspaper wrote.

Lewis and Clark County Attorney Purcell swore out the warrant for Hannon's arrest, charging him with murder in the first degree. Hannon was well liked in the Sun River country where he served as a ranch hand for a big ranch and operated a pack train for many visitors to that section.

Hannon was released on a $5,000 bond, while waiting for his trial in November. The Teton Chronicle reported on Nov. 18, 1898, "Hannon is Free. James Hannon, who shot and killed William Noel, a cowboy, at Augusta July 5 last, was acquitted of the charge of murder in the first degree in the district court Monday.

"The jury under instructions from the court rendered a verdict of acquittal without leaving the box. The state made out a very poor case from the beginning and after the third state witness had left the stand the court granted a motion of counsel for the defense for instructions for acquittal. The coroner's jury exonerated Hannon at the time of the killing, but the county attorney was determined to press the charge of murder in the first degree. The evidence all showed that Hannon acted in self-defense; that he was attacked by Noel and companions when he fired."

The Madisonian newspaper explained, "The trial of the case commenced Saturday, when a jury was secured and one witness examined. But three witnesses were examined for the state today, when it became apparent that the state was making out a very bad case. The county attorney undertook to cross-examine his own witnesses, a proceeding which the court stopped. H.S. Hepner, counsel for the defendant, moved that the court instruct the jury for the defense. This was done and the 12 men returned a verdict of not guilty without leaving the jury box."

With that incident behind him, Hannon pursued his interests again, and he was so well respected that Teton Chronicle publisher John E. Low opined that Hannon would make a great game warden for the forest district in and around the hot springs on the North Fork Sun River. "He is an old resident of that section and interested in the protection of the forest and water inhabitants. Our commissioners could not act more wisely than to make [this appointment."] That approval came in March 1899.

Hannon had a role in fingering accused murderer William Pepo who in June 1899 was convicted of killing Julius Plath in a cabin northeast of Choteau.

The Montanian newspaper reported that Pepo was shown to have attempted to cross the mountains near Hannon's cabin. He had come to Hannon's place with his pack upon his back and inquired the way over the range, the news revealed.

"Hannon had noticed the man closely because he had thought him crazy who would ask such a question. He finally directed him to retrace his steps down the river and thence south along the mountains to Cadot's Pass [Cadotte Pass]. He thought nothing more of the matter until Pepo was brought from Washington state, when it occurred to him that possibly the man he had seen might be the suspected murderer.

"When he came to town he saw Pepo and recognized him, but waited until he heard his voice in court before making the fact known to the authorities. The sound of

Pepo's voice was more readily recognized than his general appearance, which had changed slightly during confinement, and Hannon at once made his discovery known. By this testimony the state deemed the chain of incriminating evidence complete and rested."

Hannon's life in the gulch quieted for a short time. Then in February 1900, he was again under a cloud of suspicion. Hannon was accused of changing brands on 25 head of cattle, the Sun River country having been prime open range during the early 20th century.

A teaser hinting that something was amiss, was in the Feb. 2, 1900, Montanian, a Choteau newspaper.

"James Hannon was in town Friday and Saturday. There was nothing to the charges made against him at Augusta relative to his changing brands on 25 head of cattle. All who are acquainted with Hannon know that he is a perfectly square, honest man," the snippet read.

Nothing further was reported on that accusation, until on June 4, Teton County Attorney J.E. Erickson, who would later become Montana's only three-term governor, filed an information (a charge), that Hannon had illegally branded someone's cow. A bench warrant was issued for Hannon's arrest and bail was fixed at $1,000, the June 8 River Press in Fort Benton reported.

The charge read, "James P. Hannon, on or about Oct. 1, 1899, did willfully, unlawfully and feloniously, alter the brands on a certain roan cow by then and there, changing the brands 'SF,' the cow being then and there the property of E. Beach, [also spelled Beech] and not the property of the said Hannon, and being of the value of $35," with the intent to steal the cow.

According to the June 13 River Press (the Montanian was mum on the story), stock inspector Harry Lund, who was based in Fort Benton, was scheduled to testify in district court in Choteau the following week.

Fort Benton attorney F.E. Shranahan attended district court to assist the prosecution at the trial. Shranahan stated that Hannon was "a rancher living near the head of Sun River, and was accused of altering brands, the evidence in the case being secured by inspectors Preuitt of Helena, Harry Lund of Fort Benton, and W.D. Smith of Miles City. The accused was arrested in Lewis and Clark County, but on preliminary examination at Augusta it was developed that the alleged crime was committed just across the river in Teton County.

"Hannon was consequently discharged, and an information was filed against him last Monday at Choteau and a warrant issued for his arrest. The accused was in Choteau on that day and consulted counsel ostensibly in his defense. The case was set for Friday, and subpoenas were issued for the witnesses.

"The neighbors and friends of the accused refuse to believe it possible for Hannon to be guilty of the crime charged. The sheriff appears to have shared this sentiment, and in order to spare Hannon's feelings the formality of serving the warrant was dispensed with. The prosecution had 14 witnesses present on Friday, the day set for the trial, but neither the defendant nor his witnesses put in an appearance, and the sheriff is still holding the bag."

So the case against Hannon fizzled. He was mentioned on another matter that the Montanian never fully explained, except that J.G. Bair had served as Hannon's lawyer.

"Attachments were made Saturday on 14 head of cattle and five head of horses and some other property belonging to James Hannon to satisfy claims against him in favor of J.G. Bair and A.F. Bucholz. The property was brought here Tuesday and will be sold hereafter to satisfy any judgments that may be rendered," the June 15 report read.

Sheriff Hagen sold 13 head of cattle and four horses for $484. No explanation as to the different numbers was reported but Henry Jones contested the sale and he and Major George Steel claimed an unknown number of them.

On July 6, the Montanian opined, "The brave stock detectives do not seem to be over fond of trying to catch James Hannon. It is reported that one day last week six of the bold bravos surrounded his cabin at the foothills of the mountains when they thought him safely trapped, but at the last minute their nerve wilted and they were forced to leave the region without their unfortunate victim."

Hannon left the Sun River country in September 1900. He sold his cabin on the North Fork Sun River to packer and hunting guide Charles Jackson who served a wealthy clientele. He advertised in the Choteau newspapers where he came in for supplies and to meet his customers.

The Montanian newspaper in October 1903, for example, reported, "H.S. Hanson, one of the proprietors of a large publishing house at 170 S. Clinton St., Chicago, who has been in the North Fork of Sun River with guide Chas. Jackson for the past two or three weeks, on a hunting trip, returned to Chicago Wednesday evening well pleased with his trip, and loud in his praise of the North Fork as a game country. During the trip Hanson succeeded in killing three deer, two bull elk, one Rocky Mountain goat, one Rocky Mountain sheep and a grizzly bear and has taken the heads and skins of the elk, bear and goat back to Chicago with him to have them mounted."

Jackson's celebrity as a guide was short lived. In July 1902, the U.S. Forest Service named Jackson as a defendant in an action of ejectment brought by U.S. District Attorney Rasch. "The DA declares that the defendant is unlawfully in possession of about 100 acres of land on the Lewis and

Clark Forest Reserve. He asks that the government restore the land and the defendant be required to pay $1,000 damages," the Montanian noted. In other words, Jackson was accused of trespassing.

Jackson lost the property in December while his guide service was ongoing, the Choteau newspapers never going into the details. He married in December 1903 and the couple moved to Butte. By 1907 Jackson was working as a patrol driver, whatever that was.

While in Butte he killed a train robbery suspect, who was attempting to escape custody, but Jackson was exonerated by a coroner's jury. An Acantha article reported, "Following the killing of Harry Cole, a mob of about 5,000 miners at Butte attempted to lynch a detective whom they thought had done the killing, but their efforts were unsuccessful." Jackson and his family fled to Browning to take up ranching. He had married Grace Anna Armstrong, a grandchild of Teton County pioneer Jacob Schmidt. She was a member of the Blackfeet Nation, enrolled in the tribe as one/eighth Indian.

Acantha readers next got news of Jackson in 1919 when a front page story announced that Jackson had committed suicide. He left Grace with nine children the youngest of whom had only been born 10 days before. (She remarried in 1920 and the family moved to Spokane, Washington.)

But getting back to Hannon's cabin, the Rev. Haley's remarks come to mind. He said, "His cabin is neatly built and shows all the earmarks of a careful workman. The Forest Service has taken over the property, and is making good use of the hay meadows and buildings. I have seen many mountain homes both in the Rockies and the Adirondacks back home, but I have never lived in a more home-like cabin where the sun seemed to shine more friendly than here in Hannan Gulch."

By that time, Hannon's homeplace had become the Hannan Gulch Ranger Station with the spelling changed. A forest fire raged through the gulch in July 1919, but the cabin was saved "with much difficulty," the Acantha reported. Successive rangers lived at the station, monitoring the game, issuing fire permits and managing the grazing permits for 1,600 head of stock. By 1921, elk pasture had priority, with grazing permits reduced in number, thus making acres of additional feeding ground available.

Nothing is left of the old cabin and its outbuildings because the Forest Service tore them down and built a new cabin, according to the district ranger. But the name Hannan Gulch persists to mark a beautiful spot with a colorful past. ▰

Published in the Choteau Acantha April 13, 20, 27, and May 4, 11, 2022.

— 2 —

The Sheepherder's Crime

1888-1902

The press reports labeled the killing "a cold-blooded murder," but that was about all in which they were consistent in July 1888, when a sheepherder was arrested for shooting a sheepshearer in Choteau.

Choteau had been a quiet town in far western Chouteau County and the incident led to the first murder trial convened in Fort Benton in 10 years.

A mystery remains as to what date the incident happened. The Choteau Calumet newspaper published the details on Saturday, July 7, 1888, but the day and the spelling of the victim's name were later changed.

"In Cold Blood. Charles Gordon Shoots and Kills John A. LaValle Without Apparent Cause or Provocation. On Tuesday night at half-past 9 o'clock John A. LaValle was brutally murdered in front of the Choteau House by Charles Gordon. The murderer attempted to escape, but after a short chase was captured by Joseph G. Hopkinson and turned over to Deputy Sheriff H.W. Kelley, [Kelly] who locked him up and placed a strong guard on the jail during the night.

"At a hearing before Judge Garrett at an early hour the following morning, Gordon pleaded not guilty, refused to make any statement and was committed to await the action of the grand jury.

"Several respectable witnesses of the murder state that LaValle had just stepped inside the door of the Choteau House barroom when Gordon came up, called him out and raising a pistol, shot him as he approached the door, the ball taking effect under his left arm. The unfortunate man fell instantly and died in a few moments after being carried into the hotel.

"Gordon fled across Main street towards the bottom, probably hoping to reach the creek and secrete himself in the brush, but he accidentally or intentionally dropped his pistol, which Hopkinson, who was in close pursuit, picked up and turning it on the villain brought him to a standstill with the third shot. 'I didn't want to hit him,' said his plucky pursuer, who is too short and heavy for a long race, 'But I would have winged him with the fourth shot if he hadn't stopped.'

"Gordon surrendered quietly and was brought into Cohen & Silverman's store while the sheriff hunted up a pair of bracelets. It was here that more of his cool villainy became apparent. Sol Cohen recognized the pistol as one belonging to a customer and left in the store for safekeeping. Gordon stole the pistol from Cohen's desk and bought cartridges for it from W.H. Lyon, the clerk, the same evening the crime was committed. Mr. Cohen informs us that Gordon also tried to buy a gun from him on credit.

"The murderer showed no traces of drunkenness or insanity. He is a foul-mouthed wretch, refers to his crime with indifference, using the vilest language, sneers at his captors and admits that he killed LaValle because the latter refused to apologize for some fancied wrong. He is a sheepherder and has worked for S.F. Ralston during the past year.

"John A. LaValle was a sheepshearer employed by Clark Bros. & Co., and is said to have been quiet and inoffensive and unlikely to have done any man a serious wrong. He was about 22 years old and recently came from California, where it is said his parents reside. The funeral took place on Wednesday."

In the same edition, the Calumet stated, "Parties who met Sheriff Kelly and his prisoner at Freezeout on Tuesday state that Gordon has weakened considerably and begins to feel a great deal of sympathy for himself. He will probably become religious and call for bouquets and bibles when he reaches the Benton jail."

The River Press on Wednesday, July 18, wrote, "Regarding the murder which occurred at the town of Choteau Monday night last, it will be noted that neither the murderer or his victim resided in that section. They were, as usual, newcomers, and [but] for the circumstances, which led to this lamentable tragedy, the citizens of Choteau are in no wise responsible. The only wonder is that where there are so many wild and wooly loose characters constantly coming and going in a frontier town and community so few tragedies occur."

Amateur sleuths should note the first discrepancy regarding "Monday" and "Tuesday." Thanks to the telegraph, subsequent newspapers statewide picked up the story in a series of error-filled and remarkable reports using euphemisms.

The Calumet reported the story in its Saturday, July 7, edition. Other newspapers picked up the story starting Wednesday, July 11. Because of the timing of when the story ran, all other newspapers assumed the killing had happened on Monday, July 9, instead of Monday, July 2. A search found no correction in the aftermath.

LaValle's name in the later stories was changed to "LaVelle" and sometimes to "Levelle," leaving that uncertainty, too. The Great Falls Tribune on July 11 added several elements and opinions in its story, and the subsequent tellings statewide embellished the tale.

The Tribune recounted the basic facts, but misspelled the victim's name and got the location wrong, but the larger mystery was what was Gordon's motive?

"While there he appears to have quarreled with [LaVelle]. No one seems to know how the quarrel began or what it was about. Gordon apparently took offense at something and called on [LaVelle] to apologize. Whatever was said or done, Gordon went out and procured a pistol. ...

"Almost as soon as he fired the fatal shot, Gordon let fall the revolver at the feet of Mr. [Hopkinson] and fled into the street. He was caught quickly and placed in jail until yesterday when he was brought before Judge Garrett for preliminary examination. The facts were clear and the judge committed him for trial at the next term of the district court."

The papers reported that Gordon was drunk, while the Calumet in the first story said he was sober.

"He was addicted to drinking, but never got drunk while at his work. In Choteau he went on a spree as usual, and was drinking heavily on Monday when Mr. Ralston met him," the Tribune reported. "All who knew [LaVelle] spoke of him as an inoffensive man of good character. He was about 25 years old. Gordon, who is well known among woolgrowers, is about 38 years old. He was considered an industrious, hard-working fellow, who was handy on a ranch even when there was no shearing to be done."

The Dillon Tribune on July 13 added some new information. "The real cause for the killing is unknown, as no difficulty is known to have occurred between them. Apparently it was a deliberate, cold-blooded murder. Gordon, however, avers that he killed [LaVelle] because the latter would not apologize for an unmentionable insult."

The River Press in Fort Benton picked up the story on July 18, with an unusual emphasis on physical attributes.

"The prisoner, on the evidence adduced, was committed without bail to await the action of the grand jury. At 9 a.m. Deputy Sheriff Kelly was aboard the coach with his prisoner securely shackled and bound for Fort Benton via Sun River, Great Falls and the Manitoba railroad. At 9 p.m. he had his prisoner safely behind the bars of the Chouteau County jail.

"The Murdered Man. Little is known of J.A. LaVelle or his history. He came to Montana, it is thought, sometime in June from California and is said to have relatives and friends living at San Jose, California. He was a fine looking, rather tall, well-formed young man, fair complexion and light hair, and seemed to be a very clever, gentlemanly man.

"The Murderer. The River Press reporter went to the jail Wednesday and sought an interview with the prisoner. Charles Gordon is a man about five feet seven and one-half inches high, aged 32 years, weighs 150 or 155 pounds; has rather a high round forehead, straight, thin, long nose, a light crop of light-colored hair, blue eyes, chin rather full and well rounded, light-colored moustache and face somewhat pock-marked. He has the manner of a cool, deliberate and calculating man who can talk if he wants to, but can also manage to keep a [closed] mouth if necessary.

"The reporter stated his business and asked if Gordon desired to say anything relative to the tragedy, or what caused it. He at first declined to say anything about it or himself or where he came from," the report began.

The unnamed River Press reporter had unusual access in July 1888 to the accused murderer in the Fort Benton jail.

"Little by little, however, we managed to get the following points: He claims to have been born in the province of Ontario, Canada, but would not state the town; has a father, mother, two brothers, two unmarried and one married sisters living.

"Once resided in East Saginaw, Michigan, where he ran on lake and river tugs. He came to Montana in 1879 and up to last September lived in eastern Meagher County, and herded sheep and worked about sheep ranches, where he said he 'wished he had staid.' He went to the neighborhood of Choteau last September and worked for S.F. Ralston about the ranch, and afterwards herding sheep.

"Gordon's Statement. Regarding the affair, Gordon did not want to say much, but upon being told that such history of it as could be obtained from witnesses and others would be published, and that his statement would also be given if he so desired, he gradually and carefully gave the following details: He had been in Choteau, drinking more or less since the 5th of July. Two days before the tragedy he met LaVelle; had never met him before.

"They met several times during the two days, and there had been some drinking from bottles. About 4 o'clock on the evening of the tragedy, LaVelle told him he had a bottle of whiskey in Richards' stable, and they went there to drink. When there, LaVelle made an indecent and nameless proposition to him, which he indignantly resented as an unpardonable insult, and left him.

"He secured a pistol, he would not say how, and bought cartridges, with the intention of making LaVelle apologize to him. He found him as stated, and presenting the pistol, ordered him to come out and apologize. He said he did not think a lot of men would run away from a gun. When asked if he intended to kill LaVelle if he did not apologize, he said: 'No, I only intended to make him acknowledge before the town what he had done, and ask my pardon.'"

The next news report was on Oct. 17, 1888, when the River Press stated: "Gordon, the man who is in jail charged with the murder of [LaVelle] at Choteau, some time ago, seems to be getting uneasy as the fall term of court approaches.

"Jailor McNaught went into the jail Tuesday afternoon to take a look at his boarders and to see that all was going on well. The moment he stepped inside the first door he became conscious that something unusual had occurred. There were certain signs and evidences by which he divined at once that something was 'up.'

"He immediately called the prisoners to the front of their steel cages so that he could see them. All appeared except Gordon who finally emerged from a hiding place outside the cage in the main corridor of the jail. Gordon was immediately put back in the cell and securely locked in. It appears that he had, for the second time, made a key to fit the lock on his cell door and had succeeded in getting it open, and secreting himself on top of the cage outside.

"What he proposed to do next is a question. It is supposed that he intended to lay for the jailor, do him up, take the keys and make his escape and probably liberate his fellow prisoners. Mr. Gordon has by this time discovered that Mr. McNaught will not be caught napping. The key has not been found."

A week later John LaVelle's brother, William, arrived in Choteau as the date of Gordon's trial approached. He took the stage to Great Falls, then the railroad to Fort Benton as the trial commenced.

On Nov. 9, Gordon was arraigned and pleaded not guilty. The judge set the case for trial on Nov. 12. Considerable time was spent securing a jury. At the end of the two-day trial, the newspaper reported, "Able arguments were made by H.G. and S.H. McIntire for the territory and by J.J. Donnelly for the defendant. The court charged the jury upon the law and the cause was submitted. The jury returned into court at 2 p.m. and presented their verdict of 'murder in the first degree' as charged in the indictment. Sentence to be pronounced Monday, the 19th instant."

To recap, the first murder case after a hiatus of 10 years in Chouteau County (before Teton County was created) was tried in Fort Benton on Nov. 12-13, 1888.

Gordon was convicted of murder in the first degree for shooting John LaVelle or LaValle, the news reports used both spellings, in the doorway of the barroom at Choteau House on Main street, but the aftermath of the trial had twists and turns that spanned 14 years.

"Gordon pursued and shot down his victim and then attempted to escape, but was overtaken and at his trial had no defense save that LaVelle insulted him during the day," the Great Falls Leader reported.

On Nov. 19, the Leader stated, "Judge Bach today sentenced Charles Gordon to be hanged on Jan. 11, 1889. Gordon showed no emotion whatever and did not appear to realize his awful doom. Judge Bach was deeply affected as he pronounced the terrible sentence. The courtroom was crowded. ...

"The murder occurred several hours afterward and not in the heat of passion. The evidence showed the murder to have been cold-blooded and deliberate."

Although some of the Choteau Calumet editions are missing, it reported, "The Choteau witnesses and jurors attending present term of the district court at Benton are red hot because the county commissioners will only allow mileage fees for 75 miles between the two towns, while the distance by the shortest route is believed to be at least 90 miles. A number of the victims are seriously thinking of contesting the authority of the commissioners to rob them of their just dues."

The unnamed Press reporter took an unusual interest in the case, not unlike the 2015 national media spread for convicted murderer Steven Avery in Wisconsin.

"Promptly at 9 o'clock this morning a large audience was in the courtroom, it being the hour named for the sentence of Charles Gordon to be pronounced by the court. Shortly after 9 o'clock Gordon came in, guarded by Sheriff Black and jailer McNaught. The prisoner seemed in good health, his face appearing natural, full of color, and showing no evidence of the conflicting emotions within what must have been a busy brain at that moment.

"During the passing of the sentence Gordon stood upright and unmoved between his counsel, Col. J.J. Donnelly, and County Attorney McIntire. There was not the quiver of a muscle, or the slightest change in his eyes or face to indicate that he realized his awful position.

"Judge Bach was visibly affected at the nature of the stern, sad task his official duty required him to perform. It was with difficulty he could control his voice to utter the sentence, which the law required him to pass upon the doomed man. He spoke without notes for reference, and his words, ... were distinctly heard throughout the courtroom."

Bach repeated the charge and the verdict, "You maliciously, willfully, premeditatedly, intentionally and unlawfully made an assault upon one John A. LaVelle with the intent then and there to kill him, and that you did then and there by means of that assault willfully, premeditatedly and unlawfully kill and murder the said John A. LaVelle."

The judge asked, "You are now brought before the bar of this court to show cause if any you have, why the judgment of this court should not be pronounced against you. Have you any cause, sir?"

Prisoner: "I do not think that that verdict was justified in being brought in the first degree."

At one point, Judge Bach "appealed to the doomed man to retract the foul and filthy accusation against the character of the deceased as related by him on the witness stand, if that statement were false ... ," the Tribune reported, which confirmed for readers that Gordon had killed LaVelle, after LaVelle revealed that he was sexually attracted to Gordon and propositioned him.

Gordon attempted suicide in early December by cutting his arm with a piece of broken glass, but the jailor stopped the bleeding. On Dec. 15, 1888, the Press reporter interviewed Gordon again. He wrote, "The reporter left, and as he walked away this question arose in his mind: 'If Gordon's story is true, how many men are there in Montana who would not have done just as the unfortunate man did?'" Thereafter, the Press took up a cause for clemency.

Chouteau County Judge Bach sentenced Gordon to hang on Jan. 11, 1889, but at the trial and later, River Press readers learned that the victim was sexually attracted to Gordon, and Gordon responded, not with a firm rebuff, but with violence.

Homosexuality was labeled a felony crime in the past but gays existed as an invisible minority, nonetheless. Social acceptance in the West was years away. Montana did not decriminalize homosexuality until 1996.

And so the Press reporter "adopted" Gordon's cause. He turned public sentiment from "Gordon got what he deserved" into a case of justifiable homicide for which leniency was the better choice. He spelled the victim's name, "Lavalle," in the paper.

The unnamed reporter published his interview with Gordon on Dec. 19, 1888.

"During the long interview Gordon talked freely, and promptly answered every question but two, which the reporter asked him. He wouldn't tell where his parents reside, nor would he tell the name of his Choteau friend who left that place immediately after he killed Lavalle. Gordon does not look like a murderer, but the lines of his face indicate strong passions and a dogged resolution to do or to die. Yet there is nothing of the blustering bully in his manner; on the contrary, he is gentlemanly and pleasing in his demeanor and leaves the impression upon the mind of the visitor that he is a man who has mixed much among intelligent men, and that if he is not highly educated, he has at least profited by his contact with those who are."

After giving details of Gordon's appearance, and what little he would say about his background, the reporter asked, "Were you addicted to the use of liquor?"

"Yes sir, all my life, and of late years generally got on a drunk when I was where liquor could be had; yet I never had a fight or a row in my life until I was forced into this scrape."

"How did you get into it?"

"Just as I told it upon the stand at my trial. I was drinking. I never saw Lavalle until a few hours before my fatal affray with him. As I stated at my trial, he had grossly insulted me. I stole a pistol and bought some cartridges intending by a show of the loaded gun to make him apologize before the crowd. I did not intend to kill Lavalle, but the pistol went off, and he fell and soon expired. I was too drunk to run away and the world knows the rest. I expect to hang, but if it is the last word I have to say, Lavalle would not have been molested by me if he had not offered me such a beastly insult. It was a most unfortunate affair all round."

The reporter said Gordon repeated the story as he told it at the time of his trial without variation or modification whatever. "As there were no witnesses to the insult, he said he couldn't prove it, but he strongly affirmed he had told the truth and nothing but the truth in the matter."

Sheriff O'Neal sent out the customary black-ruled cards, inviting his brother sheriffs to attend the hanging, but in the same news edition mentioning the cards, was another article, "Gordon respited. The Benton murderer granted a reprieve until March 1."

"Gov. Leslie last week received an application from Charles Gordon for a commutation of sentence. ...

Preparations had already been made for the execution when Gordon asked the governor to commute his sentence to life imprisonment. As a transcript of the testimony is voluminous and has just come to hand, and as the date set for the execution is Friday of this week, the governor will not have time to review the case before that. Sufficient cause, however, appearing that the application was worthy of consideration, the governor has granted Gordon a respite and postponed his execution until Friday, March 1, which will enable him to weigh the matter with deliberation before deciding on the application. Gordon is confined to the Benton jail and has been informed of his reprieve."

Along with the news of the stay, the reporter announced on Jan. 16, 1889, that he had discovered that Gordon had been living under an alias.

Convicted murderer Gordon sat in the Fort Benton jail in January 1889 hoping that Gov. Preston Leslie would grant a commutation of his sentence from death by hanging on Jan. 11 to life imprisonment.

President Grover Cleveland appointed Leslie the territorial governor on Feb. 8, 1887, and his term was set to end on April 8, 1889. The governor granted Gordon a respite and postponed his execution until Friday, March 1. Leslie said he needed time to read the trial transcript.

Gordon had killed John LaValle as he ran into a hotel bar in Choteau in July 1888, after LaValle, a gay man, made sexual advances. An unnamed River Press reporter in Fort Benton became an advocate for leniency and published several articles about Gordon, including his real name, Charles Swanson of Dunnville, Ontario, that he discovered while doing research on the man.

"At every interview with Gordon the reporter was more and more impressed with the belief that Gordon was not the bad man at heart that he was at first supposed to be, and determined to reach the man's friends if possible. From the different interviews, he had gathered certain facts given by the condemned man concerning his family history. These were condensed and sent to the Helena Independent and thence through the Associated Press throughout the United States and Canada.

"He also wrote letters to leading stockmen for whom Gordon had worked in the Musselshell valley. Answers from Gordon's former employers spoke of him in the kindest terms, stating that his only failing was prolonged sprees at long intervals; but they had never known him in any of his drinking bouts to be at all quarrelsome; on the other hand, the man was peaceable and liked by everyone with whom he came in contact."

By Jan. 30, 1889, the newspaper had received a letter from Dunnville, stating that a petition for the commutation of Gordon's sentence was being signed by all the prominent men at that place, including the clergy, judges, members of parliament and barristers. "The petition will be forwarded to Gov. Leslie. The petitioners have known Swanson since his early childhood and all testify to his good character and peaceable disposition," the Press said.

The plan worked and Leslie commuted Gordon's sentence to life imprisonment on Feb. 14, 1889. Sheriff O'Neal took Gordon to the penitentiary in Deer Lodge a few days later.

That should have been the end of it, but in 1896, Gov. John Rickards intervened and granted a pardon to Gordon so he would be released on the day on which he reached age 50.

Then in September 1901, Gov. Joseph Toole took up the case. "The governor has the matter under advisement. Gordon shot and killed a Frenchman in the town of Choteau, which was then in Chouteau County. The defense was that he did the killing rather than participate in a nameless crime. The jury found him guilty of murder in the first degree and he was sentenced to be hanged. Preston H. Leslie, who was governor at the time, commuted the sentence to life imprisonment and has since become interested in Gordon's case," the Press explained.

The Kalispell Bee provided this summary in September 1902. "In [1888] Charles Gordon killed a man named [La-Valle] in Chouteau County, who made an insulting proposition to him, and was convicted and sentenced to hang. Three Montana governors have had a hand in prolonging his life. Gov. Leslie commuted his sentence to life imprisonment. Next, Gov. Rickards, a few days before he went out of office, ordered that Gordon should be free when he became 50 years old in 1906. Gov. Toole has finally extended a free pardon, and the pardon board approved."

The editor of the Montanian and Chronicle in Choteau wrote about the effort to free Gordon in August 1902, but by then the townsfolk had moved on from worrying about a murderer, or for that matter, the victim, 14 years earlier. LaValle (Lavelle) lies in an unmarked grave in the Choteau Cemetery.

The town of Choteau had built a small jail for $500 in 1887, where Rex's Market is located as of 2022, and Gordon spent a night there, before being taken to Fort Benton. When the Legislature created Teton County in March 1893, the townsfolk moved a building next to it to serve as a temporary courthouse. Soon the county commissioners hired William White to design a new jail, made of local stone, but that's another story.

Published in the Choteau Acantha, May 2, 9, 16, 23, 30 and June 6, 2018.

— 3 —
Wildfire
1889, 1938

The 25th anniversary of the 250,000-acre Canyon Creek Fire took place in 2013, while 2014 marked the 125th anniversary of an 800,000-acre stand-replacement fire near there.

Former Lewis and Clark National Forest Supervisor L.J. Howard, writing in the Sept. 29, 1938, Acantha, said, "Phillip Bean vividly recalls a bad forest fire in the mountains in the latter part of August and fore part of September in 1889 that burned much of the Falls Creek drainage and the North Fork of the Dearborn. Mr. Bean was then 17 years old."

Howard wrote articles for the Acantha back in the late 1930s and early 1940s about the origin of mountain and creek names in the Rocky Mountain Division of the Lewis and Clark National Forest.

Using information from the survivors of the North Fork Dearborn and Falls Creek fire of 1889, Howard said, "This fire was understood to originate somewhere near Missoula and to have burned a strip up the ridge between the Blackfoot River and the Landers Fork of the Blackfoot for two weeks to reach over the Continental Divide into the head of the Dearborn. It then continued burning for two or three days to lick up virgin timber down through the head of this watershed and over into the Falls Creek area."

Howard said Bean and his brothers had ranches in the foothills on the lower North Fork Dearborn River drainage as well as a sawmill with an overshot water wheel located a short ways above the forks of Falls Creek.

To save the mill, they backfired areas above it, and thought they had it safe, but within a day or two, a high southwest wind came up, stirring and starting the fire to spread rapidly down Falls Creek, the Dearborn drainage and some adjacent areas.

Howard continued, "The sawmill was immediately critically endangered and though the Beans attempted to save it, the fire burned and raced so rapidly down towards the foothills, up and over Steamboat mountain, then called the Dearborn mountain, and to its east slopes, that they were compelled to ride for their lives down country to their ranch at Bean Lake, thinking to try to save the buildings there and, as a last resort to save their own lives, they would take refuge if necessary in the lake itself.

"Mr. Bean described this fire as a raging holocaust that nothing could stop in the high wind that carried it along that afternoon," Howard added, noting that the foothills' vegetation was very dry. Bean described the flames from the burning timber as "leaping many hundreds of feet into the air, as jumping across creeks and gulches, up the slopes like a racehorse, and easily from mountain top to top."

As the fire made its worst run, the Bean boys ran for their lives down the Dearborn River, and as they returned to their ranch at Bean Lake, about a mile or two away from the semi-forested foothills areas, they found that settlers in the region had nearly completed burning a fire line over the open rolling prairie grasslands nearly all the way from where Augusta is today south to the foothills on the Dearborn. When the Beans arrived at their ranch in the late afternoon, the wind had died down and with the cooler evening temperature, the fury of the fire abated, Howard said. Then during the night, a three-day storm from the north, attended with a heavy rain, began that stopped the fire and practically put it out.

Howard opined that on the particular afternoon around Sept. 1, 1889, when the Dearborn conflagration raced toward and seriously endangered the stockmen's winter ranges, cinders were blown from the burning forest areas out into the prairies as much as six to eight miles to start many spot fires in the dry grass.

Published in the Choteau Acantha January 15, 2014.

— 4 —

Sugar Beet Culture Promoted But Fails to Take Hold

1892-1917

The first mention in a Choteau newspaper of growing sugar beets in Montana was in September 1891 when the Montanian reprinted this blurb.

"Capt. James H. Mills, U.S. Internal Revenue Collector, returned from an official visit to Utah, where he was summoned to inspect the immense beet sugar plant at Lehi, 40 miles north of Salt Lake, now approaching completion. Mills said the cost of the works is a quarter million and promises to prove a great success. The Utah farmers have this season a large sugar beet product about ready to harvest, and the output, it is estimated, will yield the farmers at the rate of $75 an acre. Montana aught to embark in the business."

More than 150 Montana farmers started experimenting with sugar beets that year and by October, the Board of Trade at Helena requested quantities of sugar beets for shipment to Utah to be tested for their sugar content. The board sent 18 20-pound samples. The results showed six samples had a first-class sugar content and nine samples had at least the minimum amount to be profitable.

By December 1891, the Helena Independent was regularly promoting sugar beet growing, with the hope that Helena would have the first factory for turning the beets into sugar. It reported that at a price of $4.50 per ton, the return per acre varied from $75 to $135, but with expenses the beets could be laid down at the factory for $40 per acre. It added that the first thinning required the services of one man for four or five days to the acre, coming to one man's labor caring for 10 to 15 acres.

Montanian Editor S.M. Corson first mentioned sugar beets in a report in January 1892. Choteau had a population of about 200 people at the time. "Within a radius of 20 miles of Choteau there are over 100,000 sheep, many large herds of cattle and horses; this section, of which this is the recognized center, ships over 1,000,000 pounds of wool annually, besides thousands of beeves, horses and mutton sheep.

"During the past few years several large tracts of irrigable lands have been reclaimed by water and are now ready for the farmer, awaiting only the means of transporting the product of the soil, before being made to yield up their life-giving treasures. In addition to these, there are yet thousands of acres awaiting but the 'kindly touch' to make them yield prolific crops of wheat, barley and sugar beets, besides tons upon tons of the finest hay that ever went to make up a 'cud.'"

But the sugar beet industry stalled over that "means of transporting" issue. The Helena Independent in January 1894 lamented, "Montanans, Wake Up. How much money does Montana spend every year for sugar? ... We have $2.5 million as the sum paid by Montanans every year for this one article. One or two factories in the state would not only furnish work for hundreds of operatives but profitable business for hundreds of farmers. ... When is Montana going to wake up?"

The state Legislature took a look at the problem in March 1895 and proposed a House bill to encourage beet culture and sugar manufacture. It appropriated $5,000 to pay producers a bounty of two cents a pound. By this time, the Montanian was reprinting a monthly article on sugar beet cultivation.

By then, farmers had learned a bit about its cultivation. An experiment in Nebraska showed that the distance between rows and beets played an important part, both in yield and sugar content. Eighteen inches between rows was best and the beets in the row should stand six to eight inches apart. If rows were closer it was not possible to make use of horsepower in cultivation. On smaller plots, where hand cultivation was the rule, the rows could be 15 inches apart.

The LDS church in Utah bought the Lehi plant, which had struggled financially. An article in the Montanian in July 1895 extoled the foresight of Brigham Young who "understood the merits of irrigation as an 'insurance policy.'"

While Montana farmers were reluctant to commit to commercial sugar beet culture, Idaho experimented with it in 1895. The main drawback was putting up factories to refine the sugar since the expense of transporting the heavy root bulbs long distances via wagons would diminish the profit.

Added to that, a factory required access to two million gallons of water and 50 to 75 cords of wood daily. A factory's daily capacity of beets was about 300 tons over 100 days, the produce of about 1,000 acres.

Still, the Choteau newspaper editors wrote frequently as to what a boon to the region's agricultural economy sugar beets could be. One acre would yield 11 tons, and 806 lbs. of beets could produce 100 lbs. of sugar.

"The syrup residuum can be worked into products of varying value, alcohol can be made at a high profit," the Montanian stated. The portions unsuitable for sugar could be fed to domestic animals. The newspaper figured the cost was $30.16 per acre to get the crop into the ground and up to harvesting point, then $8 additional to gather the crop.

It admitted that it was hard work to grow beets. "A gentleman who has made a study of their culture gives the following facts about them: 'This is a peculiar crop. It cannot be raised in a slovenly fashion. It means work; it means intelligent, painstaking labor. It requires a much higher order of intelligence to grow beets than it does for wheat or corn. Every acre planted in beets means 20 days' labor for one man. If two million acres of land are needed to supply this country with sugar, it follows that 40 million days' labor could thus be given to the laborers of the United States. It would also mean the transportation of 26 million pounds of freight for the industry.'"

In 1897, Montana farmers were still not sold on the venture. They were waiting for a tariff to be placed on imported raw sugar, and they also wanted the abrogation of a Hawaiian treaty on free sugar imported to the states from there. They complained that $15 million was spent on sugar from Hawaii while Hawaiians only bought $5 million in goods from the states.

In August 1902 Choteau Montanian publisher C.E. Trescott noted, "The daily papers say a sugar beet factory will soon be built at Conrad. The more enterprises of this character we have in Teton County, the better, and our citizens should do everything in their power to assist the promotions." (The Legislature did not create Pondera County from a portion of northern Teton County until 1919.)

In 1904, Trescott mentioned the proposal for a sugar plant in Conrad again, especially with the prospect of developing a vast irrigation system in the vicinity.

The Great Falls Tribune noted, "Conrad is situated 69 miles north of Great Falls, upon the Montana and Great Northern Railway; population 124. It aims to be the future county seat of Teton County. It is in the heart of a vast new agricultural valley, which is destined to become one of the greatest sugar beet growing sections in Montana, as well as nearly all other varieties of farm produce. ...

"Now while the town of Conrad is situated on the railroad and has every probability of becoming a village of a few hundred population, it is the opinion of taxpayers that changes [to] the county seat, and when that question comes to a vote, Conrad town will probably learn that the majority rules and that this majority lives in the southern part of the county."

Irrigation would be the key to bringing sugar beet culture to Teton County, and in 1906, the government's Sun River project was news. "It means the establishment of at least 1,500 new farm homes in the district, the building of beet sugar factories, creameries, potato starch factories, [and] the raising of alfalfa to feed home stock," while providing feed for the cattle kept on the region's rangeland.

Besides the beet culture, the promoters hoped that a sugar-refining factory could be built in the vicinity to defray the cost of transporting the beets to places like Billings, the Fort Belknap Reservation near Harlem and Chinook where factories were already in operation or were contemplated.

David Eccles, president of the Amalgamated Sugar Co. of Ogden, Utah, forwarded 50 pounds of sugar beet seed to Choteau to be used in testing the soil as to its adaptability in growing sugar beets. The free seed was available at Hirshberg's store in May 1906.

No news of beet culture appeared until October when H.W. Kelly and Mrs. Sabados earned first and second prize, respectively, for their sugar beet entries at the Teton County Fair. At the second annual fair in the fall of 1907, T.J. Moore and S.M. Corson earned first and second place for their sugar beet entries.

Choteau Mercantile Co. sold sugar beet seeds for 25

cents per pound, and in April 1908 the Acantha published a bulletin about the Sun River project that told of its possibilities for growing alfalfa, sugar beets and potatoes. The project was to establish a model rural village every six miles for a total of 20 communities.

In March 1909 the farmers got a reality check from representatives of the big sugar manufacturers who visited the Greenfields bench. After their visit, they stated that the land would support seven beet sugar factories, ... but it would be necessary to have 50,000 acres under irrigation accessible to a railroad before the factories would come in. Also, each factory required a farmer to contract his acreage to beets for five years.

Acantha editor A.B. Guthrie Sr. wrote about the benefits of getting a sugar beet factory in January 1913, then wrote about the benefits of getting a railroad in February. Two railroad lines were contemplated, and the Choteau Commercial Club in December 1914 pursued a campaign to secure preliminary agreements to raise sugar beets. Only 2,000 acres were signed up for beet production at first, when a minimum of 5,000 acres was necessary to support one factory.

A sugar company man arrived in Choteau in March and through his efforts signed up 6,000 acres for growing beets in 1916. But he warned that the farmers had to prepare the soil by growing alfalfa first to add humus, and he spoke of other contingencies. He said the ideal was many farmers growing beets on 10-acre plots each. Initially, they were to raise the first experimental crop on 1,000 acres to prove the country was adapted to the growing of beets on land that was near a loading station and scale.

The Acantha published conflicting information after that, but in April it listed 38 farmers who agreed to grow beets on plots from three acres to 10 acres each for a total of 285 acres.

"The acreage is spread around the territory in such a way that there will not be a person in the locality this fall that will not know something about the raising of sugar beets, and that is what the Great Western Sugar Co. wants, as their desire is to prove to the farmers that a sugar beet crop is more profitable from every standpoint that any other crop they can raise."

Planting started in May 1916. Alex Truchot was the first farmer mentioned in the news when a month later he lost all 10 acres of beets to destruction by gophers. That summer was unusually wet, and the excessive rainfall was not good for the beets. Then early cold weather did more damage and the two weather conditions "did not allow the beets to get started in very good shape, but continued hot weather of the past few weeks is bringing them out in fine shape." A sign of things to come, the article mentioned the inability to get all the hand labor which was necessary in the weeding and thinning.

However, the local newspapers in July 1916 were enthusiastic. "There is no question now but that Teton County and the irrigable territory surrounding will raise the beets, and that is all that the experiment is being made for this year. We believe there is no question but that a factory in the territory next year is a certainty."

Having seeded 300 acres in beets, the farmers by August had misgivings. A combined meeting of the Choteau Commercial Club and the farmers was held in the Farmington schoolhouse on Aug. 13. Its purpose was to get together "on the sugar beet question and to get the attitude of all the farmers on raising of sugar beets in 1917."

The Acantha printed a letter from W.L. Lawson, the manager of the Great Western Sugar Co. factory in Billings, who warned that it was up to the people to get busy.

He wrote, "Our field man, U.M. Henderson, in charge of our experimental beet growing in your territory, while thinking very well of the country and with strong faith of its possibilities, writes very discouraging letters regarding our beet-growing experiment, and reports the abandonment of a large percent of the beets planted. As you must realize, this experiment is a very costly one for this company and of vital interest to your community as the decision of this company to continue operating in your territory, will largely depend upon the success obtained this year."

After acknowledging that the weather had so far been too wet and not perfect for beet growing, Lawson wrote, "The most discouraging part of Henderson's report is that the people in different sections are losing all their interest and enthusiasm in the experiment and he fears that it will be a difficult matter to get suitable acreage another year. We are aware that the labor situation has been serious, but we have spent a large amount of money to bring labor into the country, but the communities have not been able to hold that labor in a satisfactory manner."

In a subsequent letter, Lawson said the company was willing to contract with farmers for the 1917 crop, but the farmers had to do fall plowing to prepare the soil. The Acantha urged the local farmers to "show that you are interested and willing to do your part in bringing an industry to Teton County that will do more to build up the community than any other industry that could possibly locate here."

The first meeting was not well attended, with the excuse in the paper that the farmers were extremely busy. A delegation was selected to travel to the Billings factory to talk to the farmers there and to report back at a second meeting. "All who live where they can get water with which to irrigate should attend the sugar beet meeting next Sunday," the Agawam correspondent wrote. The committee included Olaf S. Forseth, A.H. Gamble, Wm. Arensmeyer, J.W. Kerr and Chas. Suiste along with a similar committee from Simms, Fort Shaw and Great Falls.

The Aug. 23 Acantha edition devoted two and a half columns on the front page to the second meeting's discussion in Farmington.

The delegates gave "very glowing accounts" of what the sugar beet industry had done to advance the Billings territory. While the attendees were said to be enthusiastic, Henderson, an agriculturist, reminded them that the land was not in readiness for the 1917 crop. It would need fertilizer and "a lot of work to get the land clean." One must "do your plowing in the fall and do it good."

He advised farmers preparing stubble ground to use a double disk after the binder, then an irrigator to sprout all seed left on the ground, then follow with a good deep plowing to kill off about all the volunteer grain and wild oats. Henderson had other instructions for clearing land growing alfalfa.

The Acantha published the delegation's report of its Aug. 15 visit detailing the visit, and the financial details, suggesting that the same would pencil out for Teton County farmers.

Although the first large scale experiment with growing sugar beets in Teton County in the summer of 1916 was disappointing, farmers and Choteau businessmen were given encouragement from the sugar factory in Billings to try again.

The promoters reported in September, "On account of the off season this year and from the fact that much of the land that was planted with sugar beets was so foul that the present sugar beet crop throughout this locality was not the best, the Great Western Sugar Co. are preparing for another experimental crop here next year and are trying to get the farmers to make more of an effort to clean their land and have it properly prepared before planting the beets."

A Sept. 27 article on the Acantha's front page stated, "We have the land; the soil, water, and climatic conditions are found to be the best, and all that is now necessary is to properly prepare the soil.

"There should be no hesitation on the part of a single farmer to go ahead and get in shape to raise beets because if they succeed in bringing this industry into this locality, the benefits they will derive will be greater in proportion to the effort put forth than anything else than might be done."

About the same time, the Acantha ran a syndicated article about Fairfield that stated, "Next spring the waters of the Sun River will be diverted through the canals of the Sun River irrigation project to water 25,000 acres of the best land in northern Montana, situated in Teton County, south of Choteau.

"Of this acreage, about 5,000 acres will be thrown open for homestead within the next eight months. The rest of the land is already taken up long since and for several years past has been producing splendid grain crops under dry farm methods. ... It is wonderfully fertile in grain raising, and with irrigation will become one of the best sugar beet districts in the state.

"The trading point for the greater part of this district is Fairfield, one of the new Montana marvel towns that have sprung into existence almost overnight.

"Fairfield, which is less than a year old, is on the line of the Chicago, Milwaukee & St. Paul railroad. It has a bank, two stores, public garage, blacksmith shop and various other business houses. It promises to be one of the most substantial and prosperous little towns in the state."

On Oct. 11, the Acantha published a letter about the results of the 1916 harvest. "The Great Western Sugar Co.

has concluded, in what it sincerely believes to be in the best interest both of the community and of the company, temporarily to postpone the erection of a sugar factory to serve the territory."

A local factory would have been a boon for the county's development, but now the sugar company would only enter into 1917 contracts if a suitable number was subscribed, and pay $5 per ton of beets at the point of delivery at the local railroad stations after harvest. The company wanted to contract 2,500 acres of beets in the Choteau, Sun River, Valier and Conrad territories.

While the push was on to sign up growers, the Choteau Commercial Club in January 1917 awarded three prizes to farmers who raised the best crop of sugar beets in 1916. A $250 first prize went to the Northern Land Co. and the beets grown by Wm. Titmus, manager on the ranch formerly known as the Tuttle ranch near Bynum. He harvested 5.6 acres of beets that went 7.03 tons per acre.

The $150 second prize went to J.L. Hesby of Choteau and the beets were grown on the old S.T. ranch. He harvested 5.5 acres that went 4.74 tons per acre. J.E. Cashman earned the $100 third prize for eight acres of beets that went 4.63 tons to the acre.

Then came news on Feb. 21 that the Great Western Sugar Co. decided to withdraw from the territory indefinitely on account of not being able to secure large enough acreage for the 1917 crop. Grain prices were just too high for farmers to take the chance.

It wasn't until 1925 that beet culture would be tested again, near Fairfield. ▨

Published in the Choteau Acantha September 9, 16, Nov. 11, 18, and Dec. 2, 2020.

— 5 —

Indian Children Depict Washington's Birthday

1894

The 1904 Fort Shaw Indian girls' basketball team was lauded in many circles, but Choteau newspapers provided other aspects of the Indian school to contemplate in modern times. These excerpts from articles show the racist attitudes and offensive language that were common among the white population and serve as a reminder of the active, state-sponsored discrimination Montana Native Americans faced and give historical context to the Native tribes' ongoing efforts to preserve their unique cultures and traditions and to rebuild their societies that were torn apart by the white settlers.

The Montanian newspaper on March 2, 1894, reported on the George Washington's birthday program at the Fort Shaw Indian School.

"Charles Aubury, boss farmer at the Blackfeet Agency, was in Choteau last Friday on his return from a trip to Fort Shaw and Benton, where he had been looking up matters pertaining to placing Indians in school at Fort Shaw, and bringing in Indians illegally off their reserve. He had brought in with him from the agency two children whom he placed in the school on the 13th. He then went on to Benton where he found five Indians who had no permission to be absent from the reservation. ...

"Mr. Aubury attended the entertainment given at Fort

Shaw on Washington's birthday, by the pupils. The entertainment was well-attended by people residing in that vicinity. This school, under the management of Dr. Winslow, supported by a corps of able assistants, is fast getting to the front, and is ahead of some older established Indian schools.

"Dr Winslow is desirous that all his neighbors and the citizens generally visit the school, that they may see the Indian pupils at work in the various departments, where industrial work is taught, such as shoemaking, tailoring, blacksmithing and carpentering, for the boys, and for the girls, seamstress, cooking and laundry work. Music, both vocal and instrumental is also taught, and remarkable progress is being made.

"There are now 220 children in this school. Crows, Cheyennes, Sioux, Piegans and Assinaboines here meet upon a common level without danger of their scalps. Their health is good.

"Referring to the entertainment, Mr. Aubury said the school band, under the direction of Assistant Superintendent Eugene Parker, rendered some excellent music. An essay on George Washington was read by a full-blooded Piegan, Garrett Whitehorse, who, but a year ago, could not speak a word of English, demonstrated the capacity of the Indian to follow in the footsteps of the white race.

"The drill by the girls, and the rendering of the Star Spangled Banner, Columbia and America was great. The drill was under the leadership of Mary Mitchell, of Ft. Peck Agency.

"Washington's maxims were well spoken by the girls of different classes.

"The story of 'George Washington and his little hatchet' was re-enacted in pantomime by a tall Indian dressed a la continental, and a very small Indian boy; the two, representing George and his father, are in a store. George sees a hatchet and succeeds in coaxing his father to buy it.

"Arriving home, George cuts down, among other things, that immortal cherry tree, tells his father the truth about it, and contrary to the generally accepted story, gets soundly spanked for his pains, and like the boys, says he will never do it again.

"The old college song, 'Bingo,' was finely rendered by a class of large boys, and encored. A feature of the Ft. Shaw Indian School is the old-fashioned 'spelling bee,' which Mr. Aubury thinks should be recognized more extensively in our public schools than what it is.

"Mr. Aubury went north on Saturday with the Indians he had picked up at Fort Benton, though he left two of their children at Fort Shaw.

"Asked about matters at the Agency, he said everything was quiet there. No news. Under the efficient management of Capt. L.W. Cooke, acting U.S. Indian agent, the Indians of the reservation are being well looked after, and are making good progress in industrial pursuits."

Fort Shaw, an abandoned military post, was converted into the nation's 14th Indian boarding school in 1892. It closed in 1910. Every so often, the local newspapers posted the school's doings as well as brief entries like this.

"Sheriff Hagen this afternoon 'took in' a couple of young Indian runaways from Fort Shaw," posted in 1897.

"Robert Salois, Alfred Jordon and Patrick Salois, runaway pupils from the Fort Shaw Indian School, were arrested in Choteau the first of the week and taken back to the school yesterday by George Hufton," posted in 1907.

Published in the Choteau Acantha Feb. 23, 2022.

Cutting Ice

1896-1932

Ice harvesting started in January each year and the local news followed its progress through February, noting when the ice houses were filled.

The Acantha mentioned ice three times in its Jan. 30, 1896, edition.

"The cold weather of last week favored ice cutting and now the town is well supplied with material to alleviate the heat of summer.

"While cutting ice on the pond, which was supposed to be drained by excavating a new channel for the Teton, and for the loss of which pond John Jackson Sr. was paid $750 by the county, one of the workers fell in and narrowly escaped drowning.

"Strikes are the order of the day in Choteau. Last week R.M. Steele's crew of ice cutters struck, their grievance being that they were not supplied with sufficient liquid refreshments. The malcontents circulated among other crews spreading dissention, and, as a result, the supply of red fluid had to be doubled before the publicans could get their ice put up."

The people of Dupuyer were well supplied in February 1899. "Mrs. Dean has stored away 40 tons and F.D. Kingsbury and Dean & Pike have their ice houses well filled."

In Choteau, Jake Schmidt was having a large amount of ice put up, using an old log structure standing just south of the Hazlett house as an ice house.

On Jan. 31, 1902, the Montanian reported on the "only severe cold weather of the winter." The thermometer dropped to 25 degrees below zero and for a week was below the zero mark. "There is great activity among the ice harvesters as it is feared that this will be about the last opportunity to fill up the ice houses this season."

The local newspapers had syndicated articles tailored to farmers where readers learned how to cut ice, safely harvest the blocks and store them in homemade ice houses.

The annual ice harvest was reported on Feb. 6, 1908, "The ice is of the usual fine quality and purity though possibly it is not as thick as in former years. The entire crop has been taken from what is known as Miller's pond on the ranch of Wm. Miller. The 'pond' is fed by springs and partly by the Teton, being an old bed for part of the river. The harvest is a little late this year owing to the prolonged mild weather and it is not probable that there will be sufficient cold from now on to produce ice fit to put up. Last year the general break up came early in February."

The ice was cut with a saw into blocks of regular size, so that they would pack solidly into the ice house without leaving spaces between them. A regular cross cut saw, with one handle removed, answered the purpose.

Ice harvesters used a makeshift ice derrick to move the blocks. "Using a derrick a farmer can put up eight to 10 loads in two days' time, besides doing the chores at home each morning and evening," the news said.

The Adams Oil Co. cut 2,000 tons of ice from three local ponds in December 1922 and supplied Choteau, Shelby and Kevin. "Ice this year is exceptional in quality, clear and smooth and is about 17 inches thick. Mr. Adams has had a crew of 20 men at work cutting, shipping and storing for 10 days and within a day or two the ice harvest for this year will be completed."

The Farmington news in September 1929 noted, "J.B. Conner with the help of Fred W. Smith, killed a skunk in Conner's ice house last Sunday evening. The L.E. Benedict girls and Dee David Smith were spectators to the deed. Monday morning the girls went to school minus their coats and Fred's and Dee David's outer garments were flapping in the breeze on the Smith clothesline. J.B. evidently escaped unscathed, as the Conner clothesline was empty."

In January 1932, "The most severe dust storm in many years struck this community early Monday morning, doing much damage to buildings and fences. J.B. Conner's ice house, J.L. LeDesky's garage, and granaries belonging to E.J. Hirshberg and Y. Baker, were completely demolished. A granary belonging to Passmores was turned upside down and the north end of Ernest Arensmeyer's barn was completely blown out.

"Many fences loaded with tumbleweeds were blown down and scattered along the road. Moral: Next time take Premium Center's advice and raise the lower wire of the fences and let the weeds go their way."

Published in the Choteau Acantha April 11, 2018.

— 7 —

The Sun River Meteor

1897

In September 1897, Mr. and Mrs. T.A. Smith, Miss Annie Elliott and Angus Bruce left Choteau for a sojourn at the hot springs on the North Fork Sun River.

After they arrived home on Sept. 19 they stopped at the Montanian newspaper to tell Editor S.M. Corson about their remarkable adventure.

"[They] arrived home ... after a 10-days' outing at that great health resort on Sunday evening last. They found the road a hard one to travel, so much so that in places it was almost impossible to even get along on foot.

"On Friday afternoon they left the springs for home and camped that night about six miles below. Early in the evening they were greatly disturbed by a meteor, which passed over their camp at what appeared to be about a mile high and then plunged with a crash against the face of the mountain, a mile or two farther up the river. They first saw the streak of smoke and then heard the fearful crash, and felt the earth tremble as if an earthquake was upon them."

The Fergus County Argus on Sept. 22 reported that the falling meteor was a "beautiful phenomenon" in the northwestern horizon, "a ball of fire seeming suspended in the heavens for a few moments and then to fall, leaving behind a streak like that of most brilliant lightning. Several said it was the most beautiful sight they had ever looked upon."

The next day, the Dupuyer Acantha reported, "The Great Falls Tribune speaks of a meteor that fell west of that town one evening last week. The same sight was visible from Dupuyer in a southwesterly direction."

On Sept. 29, the Anaconda Standard wrote, "Great Falls. Sept. 28 — A week ago citizens residing in all parts of northern Montana noticed a huge meteor fall from the heavens, leaving a trail of smoke behind it, the like of which has never been seen here before.

"Reports coming in from all the mining districts about the state say that the great white-heated ball was plainly visible. In the Sun River district was this particularly so, and several prospectors claim that it fell but a short distance from Hot Springs. An expedition is now being formed for the purpose of searching for the body. They are now seeking information from parties who saw it, at different points as to where they believe it fell and as soon as all obtainable are in, the party will get out, headed by a man who searched for and found a meteor that fell some years ago in Iowa."

A week later, the Acantha reported that ranchers from the North Fork of Sun River country saw it fall very near the hot springs and they thought they could locate it. "Paul Bickel and Henry Lange, who are working the deposits of mineral used in the baths of the Rocky Mountain Mineral Co. of Great Falls, were at the mine and saw it fall somewhere not very distant from them. Their description of the crash which it made and the clouds of smoke which arose thereafter is thrilling.

"One old timer, who has lived in the canyon for years, came rushing down shouting that the mountain was falling over. When the seeming ball of fire hit the earth there were three distinct explosions sounding like the discharge of a battery. The earth shook and a dense cloud of smoke arose. As the gentlemen saw the phenomenon from different points of view they believe they will be able to locate the exact spot and recover the meteorite."

The Neihart Herald reported that one man was within a mile of it and saw it bursting into three pieces, with two loud explosions, "the most terrific he ever heard. ... The finder of it will be handsomely rewarded."

The last mention was in the Acantha on Oct. 10, 1897. "George I. Smith, C.S. McDonald, J.B. Kellogg and Jim Caldwell returned last Friday from a 10-days' hunt up the North Fork of Sun River. McDonald killed a black bear and the others killed some deer. They were in camp about 10 miles above the hot springs when the famous meteor fell in the mountains to the west of them. They had a very pleasant time."

No reports followed about finding the impact sites, so the pieces may still be up there. 〰

Published in the Choteau Acantha December 6, 2017.

— 8 —
Freezeout Becomes Fairfield
1907-1916

The name "Freezeout" was in use as early as June 1888 when the Choteau Calumet newspaper reported, "Road Supervisor Brown reports that several telephone poles near Freezeout have been struck by lightning. The wire, however, is not even broken and the damage to the poles is not extensive."

Researching the name, it turns out that former Choteau Acantha proprietor A.B. Guthrie Sr. had a hand in retiring the chilly reference for an old stage stop in pioneer days, and popularizing the kinder, gentler names of "Greenfields" and "Fairfield" that are references to the irrigated benchland in use today.

The government proposed using the Sun River for irrigation early in 1903 and surveying began for a ditch to the Freezeout bench. By 1906, the work had a name, the Sun River and Fort Shaw Irrigation Project.

The bench had been sparsely settled under the desert entry homesteading laws, notably by the patriarch Erastus Green, the father of 10 children, but then in June 1906 the land was withdrawn for settlement except under the provisions of the National Reclamation Act.

In July 1907, Congressman Chas. N. Pray and H.N. Savage, the supervising engineer of the Northwest in the Reclamation Service, visited the bench, and later stopped by Guthrie's newspaper office in Choteau. The conversation sparked a mission that would change the names, with the end result that by the time the town of Fairfield was platted in May 1916, Freezeout was all but eliminated as a location in Teton County. The relic name, now spelled "Freezout," remains attached to the state wildlife management area between Choteau and Fairfield that straddles U.S. Highway 89.

On July 25, 1907, Guthrie wrote, "Cut Out Freezeout. Last week when Supervisor H.N. Savage was in Choteau, he said to the Acantha, 'When I first rode over the Freezeout bench with Mr. Robbins I told him that the first thing to do in its reclamation was to change the name. A wrong impression is given by the name Freezeout, and this is especially true in the East and among prospective settlers from other states.

"'The section suffers a great disadvantage from its name. What is wanted is something strong, not deceiving and not overdrawn.' It seems to the Acantha that Mr. Savage is exactly right and that the point is one of great importance. 'Freezeout' was all right in the good old pioneer days when nobody dreamed of the place ever being settled."

Guthrie talked about sentiment, but also about names reminding people of snowballs instead of "milk and honey."

He argued, "It is barely within the range of possibility that he already has unpleasant memories of his experience in a certain game called by the same name, which it is said is sometimes indulged in by the residents of certain sections in the East. Or maybe he hails from the snowbound woods of northern Minnesota or the bleak plains of the Dakotas on which the Chinook does not smile. Either way he has had all of the Freezeout proposition that he cares for. It means in one case an empty purse; in the other, of frosted cow chips, twist straw, chop jack pine and of other ways to keep his blood flowing.

"Freezeout? Nay, nay! Nothing doing. The word is a

misnomer and a slander. Freezeout flat is not as frigid as its name by half the length of the thermometer. Anybody who has lived in this country or even been here knows all about our mild late falls, and about our winters tempered by the Chinook winds.

"Freezeout is exactly the same so far as climate goes as other parts of Montana lying at the base of the east slope of the Rockies. It is not a rigorous climate at all. Barring changes, which are sometimes sudden, it is really a climate with many advantages. Why then bring the country into ill repute by misnaming it?

"And remember, there is often a great deal in a mere name. It is time to cut out 'Freezeout.' In the words of Mr. Savage, what we want is something strong, not false, and not overdrawn. The truth about that empire of fine land is all that is needed. There is no necessity of stretching it at all.

"In the end no doubt, the reclamation service or the post office department will solve the difficulty by simply clapping some name, or other on the place, but the Acantha has a plan for naming it just the same. It is this," Guthrie began.

"For six weeks or two months, this paper will receive suggested names. These will be published as they come in and when there are no further names sent in, a voting coupon will be printed in the paper and all subscribers may register their choice by mailing their votes to the Acantha. For the name receiving the highest number of votes, the Acantha will give $5, for the second choice, $3.50, and for the third, $1.50. So go for it. Send in the names at once. There will be no limit on the number any one person may send. Don't put the matter off until your enthusiasm cools. The proper time is right now. Further details as to the voting will be given out later on. Come on with the names. Let's rechristen Freezeout."

During August 1907, the Acantha published the names in the order they were received in the news office, and by Aug. 29, readers had submitted 51 names. The name, "Fairfield," was the 13th submitted and "Greenfields" was the 29th.

A ballot was published and after the Sept. 18 poll deadline, the Acantha had tallied 352 votes for Greenfields, 35 for Good Hope, 35 for Bison, two for Goodenough and one for Argile Bench. Fairfield was not in the top three. (New subscribers upon payment of subscriptions in advance could cast 35 votes, instead of one, for each subscription.)

The Acantha explained, "The first name and the winner was suggested by S.M. Corson, [editor of Choteau's former rival newspaper, the Montanian] though the same name was suggested a little later by Mrs. J.W. Ward of Belleview. Good Hope was suggested by Rev. George Logan, and Bison by Mrs. P.O. Nasse.

"Greenfields is easily the favored name as the vote attests. As we said at first, it is very difficult to change a name established by custom. The results of this vote may result in the bench being called Greenfields or it may not. It is hardly necessary to say that no one can be compelled to call it so. The post office authorities will probably determine the matter in the end.

"We feel that Greenfields is a good name. It is euphonious, not too long, and there is probably not another post office of the name in the United States.

"The name is not overdrawn and it carries no unpleasant suggestion. It is true to conditions as they are and as they will be when the bench is settled; moreover, it does honor to one of the very earliest settlers of this section, a man worthy of our respect and honor, Erastus Green, who for many years was a resident and about the only resident of the country to which the name applies.

"As a mere name it is certainly better than Freezeout. Until the matter is settled authoritatively, this paper will call the bench, 'Greenfields,'" Guthrie wrote.

The irrigation project engineer told Guthrie that they liked the name, Greenfields, although they each had their own suggestion.

The community's petition for a new post office was completed in November 1907, but there we have a mystery that might be explained elsewhere, as the Acantha offers no details.

In March 1908, Guthrie wrote, "Through the efforts and influence of Congressman Pray, in answer to a petition of the residents, a new post office to be known as Fairfield has been established on the Sun River bench with John Zimmerman as postmaster. The people of that section formerly got their mail at Choteau and the new office will prove a great convenience.

"The name was selected from a list of three which were submitted, and while some of the patrons interested would have preferred the name Greenfields, it was not chosen. That name, however, is beginning to be quite generally applied to the entire bench, and may establish itself for that use. Other post offices will be established on the bench as it settles up and Greenfields may also be the name of one of these later on."

In May 1911, Guthrie wrote about "considerable rumpus" raised over the recent change of names of Montana mountains and streams by Forest Service officials. He mentioned "our old friend Freezeout" and reflected, "Names change, sometimes for very good reasons, and again for reasons unknown or no reason at all."

On May 29, 1916, Elmer Genger & Co., platted the Fairfield townsite several miles to the south of the old post

office on the route of the Milwaukee Road line, thus ensur-
ing the name's survival to this day. ▰
   Published in the Choteau Acantha June 1, 8, 2016.

— 9 —

A Frigid Winter

1909

The spate of extremely cold weather through December 2016 and in the first two weeks of January 2017 came close to the record cold weather in January 1909.

"In the Embrace of Winter," wrote Acantha Publisher A.B. Guthrie Sr. on Jan. 7, 1909, after receiving the daily temperatures from voluntary weather observer Herman Van De Riet, a farmer in Farmington, about six miles northeast of Choteau.

"Since Sunday this section of the county has suffered extreme cold weather. The same is true of all other parts of the county, and for that matter of the entire Northwest. There has not been much snow, perhaps three or four inches in all.

"On Tuesday the wind was from the west, and although extremely cold, there was a chance for moderation; but it swung around to the north again and has stayed there since. The lowest temperature was reached early Wednesday morning when recorded was 40 below.

"So far there has probably been no great injury to livestock, as there is an abundance of hay for the emergency. Stages have run as usual, except that the Dupuyer stage failed to make the trip today, on account of snow badly drifted in the coulees. It is snowing harder this afternoon, and the fall promises to be very heavy."

A week later, Guthrie wrote, "Monday forenoon there was a decided change made from the extremely cold weather, which had prevailed for a week and a day preceding. The thermometer rose rather rapidly to zero and was above that temperature most of the time until Tuesday evening.

"The recent cold spell is one of the most severe that has been experienced here. Two years ago the cold held on much longer, but the temperature did not go so low.

"So far as reported there is little or no damage to livestock to date. Stockmen and ranchers are feeding heavily, but there is an abundance of hay. ... Snow has fallen to a depth of about a foot, most of it having fallen last Thursday night.

"Monday night a strong wind blew for a short time and drifted the snow badly in places, making the roads bad for traveling. Tuesday night the cold increased and Wednesday a blizzard was on until evening. Today it is bright, but cold."

Guthrie then listed the low temperatures Van De Riet had recorded for Jan. 1-14, 1909: -5, 8, 5, -20, -35, -40, -32, -31, -30, -42, -26, -15, -17 and -30, respectively.

Guthrie added, "For a few days during the cold weather the janitor at the high school building found it difficult to make the rooms sufficiently warm, and it was found necessary to dismiss the pupils for about a day and a half. The difficulty was overcome by installing another radiator, and the building was made comfortable even before the warmer weather set in."

Finally, on Jan. 21, Guthrie reported that a Chinook wind had arrived. "Overcoats, gloves, fur caps and overshoes have not been a necessity since last Friday. Frozen ears and noses have had a chance to thaw. The coal pile has not wasted away so rapidly and it has been possible to sit away from the stove even when the fire was low.

"The reason for this change is that the Chinook came gently down upon all this section of country Friday morning. The temperature rose from about 16 below at 8 o'clock to 34 above at 10, a rise of 50 degrees in two hours. While the Chinook has not been of the warmest kind, it has blown almost continuously since it began, and the thermometer has hardly stood below the freezing point, and then only for short periods. The thaw has been general and slow, which is all the better for stock, range and crops. The cold spell held on for 12 days, and the relief afforded by the warm weather is a matter for thanksgiving. Sunday night it rained in Choteau for a while, and Tuesday it was raining at Saypo and along the mountains, a soft, warm, summerlike rain."

The weather improved but the Teton County pioneer stockman and patriarch, Auguste Francois Truchot, 75, as well as the youngest addition to the large Van De Riet family were not to see it. Truchot died on Jan. 10 after a short illness and Herman's grandson, Simon, an infant but a few months old, died on Jan. 13 of whooping cough complicated with pneumonia.

Published in the Choteau Acantha Jan. 18, 2017.

— 10 —
Friend Zimmerman
1912

Friend Roy Zimmerman, born in 1887, was a young man who showed leadership qualities from an early age.

Born to John Zimmerman, a businessman, Fairfield's first postmaster and Teton County's first elected sheriff, and his wife, Eva, Friend excelled in grammar school and high school, where his father was a school trustee. On May 22, 1906, Friend, the class president, graduated in a class of nine at the fourth commencement of the Teton County Free High School, the largest class to graduate in the new building at that time.

The fresh-faced young man and his classmates were pictured on the front page of the Choteau Acantha, which noted that the commencement audience was the largest ever assembled under one roof in Choteau. His many brothers and sisters (10 children) were likely as proud of him as were Friend's parents.

On May 31, the Acantha published the graduates' essays. Friend's theme was on the "Aristocracy of Character."

He said many kinds of aristocracies existed, based on birth, wealth and intellect, for example, but the finest and truest was the aristocracy of character. "It excludes no one because he is not wealthy; no one because he has not a perfect mind and no one because he has not a legacy of a long line of ancestors. It cannot be destroyed, nor affected by wars or invasions, and no person in this aristocracy can claim a title without deserving it.

"Character is power in a much higher degree, than knowledge is. Mind without heart, intelligence without conduct and cleverness without goodness are powers, but powers that may be only for mischief."

He ended the essay, saying that there is more aristocracy in "one forgiving smile, than in all the pretensions to worthiness in the society of the mean and vulgar."

By October 1907, Friend, 20, had moved from being a salesman at the Choteau Mercantile to a job at the local mill from where he traveled around the county and to Great Falls on business. He found time to remove carcasses where needed around the county, receiving $5 each. He assisted in voter registration around the county earning $9.50 a month. He found time to hunt and he homesteaded on the Fairfield bench, intending to take up farming.

And then it was over. The Acantha on July 11, 1912, reported, "What was perhaps the saddest and most shocking accident that has ever happened in Teton County occurred Sunday morning at about 9 o'clock, near the Barrett crossing on Deep Creek, some 25 miles west of Choteau, when Friend Zimmerman, aged 24, son of John Zimmerman and wife, pioneers of the county, was shot and instantly killed as the result of an accidental discharge of a 22-caliber target rifle in the hands of Miss Mabel Zimmerman, a sister of the victim.

"A party of young people from Fairfield were spending an outing at the Deep Creek canyon, and on the morning of the tragedy, just before breaking camp to start for home, it was proposed by Friend, who had been even more than usually cheerful throughout the trip and a leader in the pastimes of the party, that a few shells which he had left in his pocket be used up.

"He went a few steps forward and was in the act of stooping to pick up a discarded tin can to be used as a target. As he did so, his sister picked up the gun, which had not yet been fired. In a flash, the rifle exploded, and Friend fell forward. It required a moment for the members of the party to realize the awful truth, but a telephone message was sent almost immediately from a neighboring ranch house to Choteau for a physician, in the hope that Friend was only unconscious. It was soon realized, however, that he was dead, and it is believed that death was instantaneous this being indicated by the fact that the body never stirred after falling, and the further fact that the bullet entered at the base of the skull behind, and pierced the brain.

"The condition of the sister at the time of the accident was most pitiable, and has remained such as to cause much anxiety to her family and friends," the Acantha reported.

It described the funeral, the profound sorrow in the community, and ended with, "He was by nature, as by name, friendly. He accepted life's responsibilities cheerfully as they came, and discharged them faithfully. And this means that his life was a success."

Mabel, 17, recovered, helped by the community. She married William Crittenden in 1915 and they moved to Seattle in 1937. She died in 1978 at age 83.

Published in the Choteau Acantha Nov. 9, 2016.

— 11 —

Gophers

1915

As pests go, the Richardson's ground squirrel, commonly called a gopher, has been a favorite target in Teton County since as least 1910.

The Drake Drug Co. ad in the July 14, 1910, Acantha read, "Use Our Kill Em Quick for gophers and our pure insect powder for flies. Prescriptions carefully compounded."

By March 1913, the Sunnyside Store Co. in Power was also promoting the chemical and the Acantha's syndicated newspaper pages routinely offered advice to farmers about the critters.

Rodenticides were widely sold by 1913 and they were especially promoted in the early spring when the gophers emerged but green-up had not yet occurred. Strychnine-laced oats were the best bait to seed around the burrows.

The Choteau Drug Co.'s ad in March 1913 read, "Now is the time to poison the gophers. Woodlark Squirrel Poison, one pound cans, 35 cents; three for $1. We also have a fresh supply of strychnine."

Later in June the Choteau Mercantile Co., with the logo, "The Busy Store," suggested, "Why not get a 22 rifle and combine a little sport with your work when you go after those gophers? Or else get a can of Woodlark Squirrel Poison."

The first long article on gophers appeared on March 4, 1914. "Band together to kill the gophers. The farmers of the Porter bench country [northeastern Teton County] have organized and are preparing to take concerted action in killing off the gophers in the spring." It said every farmer in the district was taxed a small sum to purchase strychnine, which was used together with wheat, "and is said to be sure death to the gophers. Mr. Thayer was in Conrad and obtained some that will be distributed along with instructions," the Acantha reported.

By October 1914 four different gopher-killing products were on the market locally, and in somewhat of a disconnect, the "Gopher" brand name was as ubiquitous as Heinz or Campbell's with the sale of cans of Gopher sauerkraut, spinach, tomatoes and pumpkin, among others, available on store shelves at E.J. Roberson & Co.'s "Cash Store."

As the Fairfield community's agricultural production ramped up in the spring of 1915, the local correspondent advised, "The spring brings with it more gophers than ever before, so it is the duty of every farmer to get busy and help exterminate them. Available at Mac Vicar's."

The Acantha was on a tear on March 31, 1915, when it railed against alleged inferior gopher-killing products. "The cupidity of manufacturers has, in many cases, led them to diminish the amount of poison below the safety point, with the result that it has proven worthless in use. Use well-tried, tested brands of coated wheat.

"These rodents are now awakening; soon, with the warm sun's rays, their whistle will be heard, and this is the psychological moment to sprinkle the poison wheat. A few grains in the early morning, dropped down each burrow, will turn the trick. The long fast makes the creatures ravenous and the poison is immediately effective," the newspaper opined.

The Fairfield and Bole communities were the first locally to use the phase "Gopher Day," when the Farmers Equity, the precursor to a cooperative, hosted a meeting in April with three speakers at the local Grange hall to launch a campaign to get rid of gophers.

On Sunday, July 18, 1915, the first Gopher Day occurred, wherein the farmers of the Bole country agreed to pay one cent a tail for every tail brought in to the farmers' hall on that day. A baseball game was planned along with races "and other amusements in which both men and women can take part. You are all invited to attend," the local correspondent said.

The successful event was reported the following week under "Bole items. Gopher Day was quite a success in spite of the big rain Saturday. About 300 people attended the celebration." They counted 4,000 gopher tails, and the total payout was $38.65 "to our ambitious boys."

Maurice Hans got the 22-cal. rifle for having the largest amount of tails. Robert Brennan won the second prize of six gopher traps and the third prize pocketknife went to Ernest Larson.

"The gopher population has been considerably decreased by the efforts of the children," the local columnist said, and the Rogers-Templeton Lumber Co. was thanked for the prizes.

The government's war on gophers enlisted young boys in the effort.

The Farmington School teacher, for example, announced in April 1916, that the scholar who garnered the most gopher tails by the end of the school year would receive a prize. On May 24, Otto Arensmeyer was declared the winner.

Choteau's Commercial Club met in May to decide whether to have a Good Roads Day, a Gopher Day or a 4th of July celebration. An organized Gopher Day fizzled, although two Gopher Day captains were appointed, C.A. Cowell and C.S.

McDonald, as proposed leaders of opposing sides, the team tallying the lesser number of tails to pay for a banquet.

The news of war in Europe filtered into Choteau after 1914, and the powers that be, adopted that term for the gopher fight in March 1916, when one supplier revised its poison ad: "War should be declared immediately upon the gopher. Now is the time to use poison most effectively. We have a fresh stock of strychnine, Woodlark and Carbon Disulphide. Choteau Drug Co. Oldest drug store in Teton County."

J.M. Davis, the county agriculturalist, published a front-page article, "Destroy the Gophers," in the June 14, 1916, Acantha edition, noting for the first time in the press that the loss of natural predators might contribute to the gopher increase.

"The homesteaders and ranchers have trained their guns on the coyote, hawks and owls, and snakes have been destroyed till at present most of the gophers' natural enemies have been made way with. ...

"It is claimed that every pair of gophers now will destroy one to 1.5 bushels of wheat besides the grass, corn and garden stuff they dig up, eat off and destroy. Several farmers over the country have awakened to the situation and are now scattering poisoned grain and making great inroads upon their numbers as may be seen by the dead ones found along the roads and fences and over the fields."

Davis provided the formula for soaking strychnine with wheat kernels and ended his pitch with, "Go after them, declare war on them as they are entrenched all about you and will not agree to terms of any kind, so it is up to us to annihilate them. Go after them, get them no matter how, but get them. Anything is fair in modern warfare."

Davis continued his war language with, "Every man and woman should consider it a patriotic duty to assist with the work," while the Acantha noted that local farmer Alec Truchot had lost 10 acres of sugar beets to gophers in August 1916.

The state Legislature responded in March 1917 by passing a law authorizing counties to levy taxes and employ agents to exterminate the gopher pest. "The purpose of this campaign is to demonstrate the benefit of such a wholesale extermination method," the Acantha stated, adding that the federal government would assist the local county agents by assigning a federal biologist who would spend the spring and summer months in Lewis and Clark, Teton, Fergus, Cascade and Hill counties.

In April 1917, the same month that the United States declared war on Germany, an ad for poison labeled gophers as "Pro-German."

County Agent W.S. Murdock asked the Teton County commissioners for a $200 appropriation (about $4,078 in today's dollars) to be used for the purchase of poison, so he could prepare the strychnine-wheat/oats mixture and furnish it to farmers at a cost of about 14 or 15 cents per pound. He said one pound of poison was enough for 20 gopher holes.

Murdock wrote a long article titled, "Exterminating the Gophers," in April where he followed Davis's lead in using war-related language. He chided "thoughtless gunners" who were killing the gophers' natural enemies, saying, "Give them the benefit of the doubt. They are not all bad, even if a few, like some of the human race, acquire habits, for there are good and bad individuals and species among the wild animals, and some nicety of discrimination should be applied to them as is given to the human species."

Murdock predicted that in the next few years, farmers could completely exterminate the gophers in the county by organizing poison-mixing gatherings to make enough poisoned grain to place one teaspoonful at 240,000 gopher holes. He planned to set up demonstration plots next to roads for passers-by to see the dead carcasses and how effective the war was. Alas, the first war casualties were horses.

The Acantha reported in May 1917 that James W. Gray, who lived south of the county line near Crown Butte, at a place called Riebeling, lost three horses that week from poisoning.

"He had poisoned oats that he intended using for gophers in the back of his buggy, and sometime during the night the horses got at the poisoned grain. This should be a warning to all farms to be careful and not put the poisoned grain where stock have access to it," the Acantha opined.

Bole had its second annual Gopher Day on June 19, 1917, and that fall, the Teton County commissioners approved spending $3,000 for strychnine and other ingredients.

The Legislature ramped up the gopher-killing campaign in February 1918 with a new law, which Teton County put into effect on March 1, that compelled farmers and landowners having infested land to put out gopher poison, and if they refused, the county's gopher poisoner would "upon 10 days written notice enter upon any farm, railroad right-of-way, grounds or premises where there are gophers and poison, kill and exterminate them, the cost to be charged against said land and may be collected the same as taxes."

The big spring gopher extermination campaign commenced whereby poison was sold for 15 cents per pound in cloth bags in three sizes, 10-, 20- and 30-quart sacks stamped "Poison" in large letters. On that basis, there was no danger of forgetting what is in the sacks, the Acantha reported.

Ten tons of oats laced with one half ton of strychnine went out to Teton and nine central Montana counties. "It's the farmers' common enemy and the Kaiser's best friend in the west," an ad read.

"He strides out into the infested field right into the front little trenches of his worst enemy and with a little caution he hurls not the Mill's bomb [the name of the first hand grenade], but the gopher poison on the top of the trenches where the enemy comes for food. War has been declared now; each farmer do his part and this campaign is going to be a grand success. Bring back bags to be refilled," the Acantha stated.

On March 21, 1918, the Teton Slope schoolboys of the Loyalty Club, the Junior Red Cross, "believe they can show their patriotism in no better way than killing gophers, so in addition to their regular work they have killed 85 of the pests."

The next week the school's gopher count was up to 197. "This means 197 bushels of wheat saved for Montana," the Acantha reported.

The Acantha intoned, "War! All is war! Every paper you pick up is filled with war, for war causes war. In Teton County war has been declared against the gopher because he is one of the greatest crop-destroying agencies in this county."

More poison meant more collateral damage. On May 2, 1918, George W. Porter, of the Porter Bench, reported that "through the carelessness of someone putting out gopher poison" he lost a 4-year-old colt. The person had put the poison on top of the hole instead of just at the mouth of the hole, "and in such big quantities that the horse ate some and succumbed immediately. Many jack rabbits can be seen stretched out on the prairie dead from the results of eating gopher poison," the Acantha stated.

In July M. O'Neil of Agawam lost six horses by poison. "He went to the Montana Elevator Co. for feed oats and the man in charge sold him some that were doctored for the gophers."

By the start of 1919, the county was spending more than $1,000 per month in the spring on gopher extermination. For example, the commissioners in April approved a $50.80 payout to Harold Lindseth for wages for mixing poison. The state contributed 1,000 pounds of "government poison" for use on leased and unleased state land.

As the Great War wound down in the fall of 1919, the gopher extermination campaign, under the leadership of Chas P. Crane of the Teton County Farm Bureau, was ranked as one of the largest campaigns put on in the state.

Between 600 and 800 people attended the July 1919 Teton County Farm Bureau picnic, where Crane was elected the leader of gopher extermination.

By October, according to an Acantha news report, the bureau's gopher extermination campaign, with the cooperation of the county commissioners, "ranked as one of the largest campaigns put on in the state. Teton County ranks second in the amount of strychnine used, amount of poison mixed, and amount of land covered.

"It would have been a great saving had there been any crop to save. Even though the saving was not so great this year, we know that through this work a great many gophers have been destroyed and they will be less troublesome in future years.

"Teton County last year used about 30,000 pounds of poison on 300,000 acres of land. Next year this work will be carried on as usual according to plans now being drawn up by those Farm Bureau members who took an active part in the work last year."

The Acantha's reference to failed crops was explained in a June 26, 1919, report that stated, "Taken as a whole, indications point to what may be regarded as a crop failure and which marks the third successive failure suffered by the farmers of this particular section of Montana after the bumper crops of 1915 and 1916, and which will result in hardship to a great many of them who had staked their all on the prospect of a good crop this season."

While the farmers sought federal aid in the months after World War I ended, they continued to kill gophers under pressure from the county fathers. A legal notice in March 1920 stated that everyone was notified to poison gophers on their land between March 29 and April 3. "In case they fail, the county exterminators will immediately proceed to poison the gophers on said land and the expense thereof will be charged against said land's taxes for the year 1920. Signed Chas P. Crane, E.D. Forrest and R.D. Anderson, commissioners."

Extension Agent Robert Clarkson did his part, distributing 2,800 pounds of poison for use on state land and he offered an especially "high power" gopher poison to the people living next to the mountains where lived a "large brown gopher." One wonders if that was a reference to a marmot population or to the west-side's Columbian ground squirrel, the cousin of the Richardson's ground squirrel that was the scientific name for the east-side pest.

"The ordinary gopher poison prepared by the county is not strong enough to kill this particular gopher and a special mix must be made for this poison," the Acantha reported.

Choteau Mayor J.C. Morgan in May at the county schools track meet offered $10 for the boy or girl who brought in the greatest number of gopher tails and $5 for the second largest number. Clarence Bjork won with 260 tails and Dalmas Staley was second with 134.

Clarkson and the Farm Bureau continued the gopher war for the next decade and in all that time only one dark moment clouded the campaign.

In April 1926, former Collins farmer Ole Quenemoen,

73, who with his wife had been making his home with their daughter, Mrs. W.L. Andrews, about two miles east of Power, had been poisoning gophers on Monday, according to the story told to Sheriff Collins and Coroner Connor, who were called to the Andrews ranch at 4 p.m. Tuesday.

Monday morning the Andrewses went to Great Falls and some time later Mrs. Quenemoen went to a neighboring ranch, so the old man was alone at home from about 10 a.m. until 3:30 p.m. when the family returned to find him dead in his bed.

"On the stove was a gallon pail, similar to pails in which syrup is sold. The pail was about a quarter full of poisoned oats and liquid and a bowl partly filled with the liquid was found on the kitchen table, with a spoon beside it.

"The old man's body was found on the bed where he had died, to all appearances, without any struggle. He had removed his shoes and looked as if he had simply fallen asleep.

"Despondency over ill health is thought by relatives to have prompted the old man's act. He had threatened to take his own life before during periods of ill health, they said." He was buried in Farmington Cemetery.

Published in the Choteau Acantha Feb. 8, 15, 22, and March 8, 2017.

— 12 —

Hunting Tragedy Mars Thanksgiving

1920

Simms rancher James Phillips and his foster son Charles Torrance set out to hunt near the Sun River Hot Springs during the Thanksgiving week of 1920.

Experienced with guns, the news reports show, Phillips had had a reckless encounter in 1910, and Torrance had survived the war in France in 1917-1918.

Phillips and his wife Cora informally adopted Charles as a young boy when they lived in Vandalia, Illinois. By 1910 the family had settled near Simms on the north side of the Sun River, the boundary between Teton and Cascade counties.

In June 1910 James Phillips made the news when "in a quarrel over a piece of land on Sun River over near Lowry last evening, Harry O. Beale, [age 30, assistant superintendent and civil engineer for the U.S. Reclamation Service] near that point, was shot through the right arm by J.A. Phillips, a rancher living near the same place.

"Beale is now a patient at the Deaconess Hospital and Phillips is held at the county jail. At the jail Phillips stoutly maintained his innocence, and stated that he shot in self-defense. According to his story, the trouble has been brewing for some time, and first arose over the fact that both men claimed the right to the same piece of land."

The Acantha reported after the October trial in Choteau,

"The case was stubbornly contested by the ablest legal talent on both sides. The jury sent Phillips to the county jail for six months."

Torrance, born in 1893, enlisted in the U.S. Army in 1917 from Illinois. He became a private in the 119th Field Artillery Regiment, Battery B, according to several reports, and after serving in France, and surviving a gas attack, he came home to Simms in May 1919 to work on his father's farm and ranch.

Three newspapers reported on what happened at the Hot Springs, the Great Falls Daily Tribune having the most details. Only the Acantha got Charles's name spelled right, "Torrance," while the others spelled it, "Torrence."

"Special to the Tribune. Gilman. Nov. 25. Victim of a souvenir which he picked up on the battlefields of the Argonne while serving under the U.S. colors, Charles L. [Torrance] lies dead in this place, his body having been brought here this morning from a hunting camp at Hot Springs on the North Fork of the Sun River in the Rocky Mountains.

"Torrance, who was about 27 years of age, was engaged in a hunt in company with his foster father, J.A. Phillips, of Simms. Late Wednesday evening Torrance was working around the cook wagon when a pistol, which he was carrying in a pocket of his shirt dropped to the ground. He picked it up and later the pistol again fell out, this time being discharged and the bullet passing through Torrance's chest. He died in about 40 minutes.

"The body was brought to Gilman this morning and the sheriff and coroner of Teton County were notified, they coming here late this afternoon to conduct an investigation.

"Young Torrance had resided at Simms for a number of years and was single. At the beginning of the war he had enlisted in the U.S. Army, serving in France in the 119th Field Artillery. He took part in a number of engagements and was gassed. While in the Argonne he found a pistol in an abandoned battle tank on the field and brought it back to America with him. It was this pistol which caused his death."

On Dec. 3, 1920, the Choteau Montanan reported, "The funeral of the late Chas L. [Torrance] ... was held at the Methodist church in this city by Rev. Harry T. Stong, the pastor, under the auspices of the American Legion, the pall bearers being M.C. Martin, T.O. Kikosh, H.D. Swanson, Victor Steele and J.O. Nelson. The color bearer was Chas. Dollemore, while Floyd Churchwell and Jack Rigler were the color guard, and Nick Pambrum the bugler. The burial was made at the Choteau cemetery." James and Cora put a card of thanks in the paper and made sure that a white marble (Veterans-Administration-issued type) tombstone marked Charles's grave. ▨

Published in the Choteau Acantha November 25, 2020.

— 13 —

Reservoir Deaths

1923

Large bodies of water draw big people, just as puddles do toddlers, but water can be a killer, as the Acantha has reported over the years.

After its concrete retaining wall was built in 1916, Bynum Reservoir, located about six miles west of Bynum, started filling with water, fed by a diversion dam and canal at the Teton River several miles to the south.

The first drowning was reported in the Nov. 29, 1923, Acantha. Ted Ellis, 34, an African American from Great Falls, married with three children, and a buddy, fell out of a boat when a windstorm came up while they were duck hunting.

"The first intimation those on shore had that anything was wrong was when E.O. Berry, member of the party, started to drive around the shore of the reservoir after he had finished eating his lunch. He saw the overturned boat, S.G. Evens clinging to it. Berry rescued Evens, who said that Ellis had gone to the bottom nearly a half hour ago. After first aid was rendered, Evens was taken to the Ed. Bailey ranch, where he was put to bed and in a few hours was in shape to be taken to Great Falls.

"Efforts of the hunters to bring the body of Ellis to the surface were unsuccessful and the local sheriff's force were at once notified, who in turn notified Deputy Sheriff Curt Dennis, of Great Falls, with the request that he bring up grappling hooks from the county jail. Due to the fact that the exact location of the accident is hard to determine and the large amount of weeds and brush (and trash) in the bottom of the reservoir, grappling proved to be a hard proposition, and the work was abandoned when darkness came, with the intention of resuming the work on Monday morning," the Acantha reported.

Teton County Sheriff William Reiquam and Elmer Cardell tried again on Monday, but were unsuccessful, and then the search was abandoned when the body of water froze over. The Teton County commissioners, the Dec. 13 Acantha reported, agreed to pay a $100 reward for the recovery of Ellis's body.

The April 18, 1924, Acantha brought the news that two boys walking along the shore of Bynum Reservoir found Ellis's body which had washed ashore after the ice thawed. The unnamed youths got the reward.

Eleven years later, the Oct. 31, 1935, Acantha reported, "Sunday while hunting ducks on the Bynum reservoir, H.M. 'Babe' Snider found a 32-20 Savage rifle lying in the mud some distance off shore. The weapon was disclosed to view by the present low condition of the water in the lake, and was found on the northwest side of the lake about halfway between the east and west ends.

"There is some conjecture as to what might have caused the gun to be lost there, but the one which is considered quite probable is that it was in a boat which capsized on Nov. 25, 1924, and resulted in the drowning of Theodore Ellis. ... Several years later a shotgun was found when the lake was lowered and the rifle just found is thought also to have been in the boat. It was in a fair state of preservation and Mr. Snider believes it can be made to shoot again."

The front page Acantha photo on Jan. 17, 1946, showed Sheriff Albert Peterson and Undersheriff Earl Hollar sitting in a boat above the exact spot where brothers Sam, 45, and Tayfield Becker, 31, of Fairfield were believed to have drowned in Bynum Reservoir.

"The two brothers first were missed yesterday when a searching party followed faint car tracks to the open channel pictured above. The car is visible some 12 feet below the surface of the water. Hoists today may bring the vehicle to the shore, which is about 600 yards away from the spot."

The men had been perch fishing at the reservoir and were believed to have gotten lost. They drove out on the lake on the south side and into a 20-foot open channel with a 1936 model Chevrolet, which sank to the bottom of the lake head first and ended up nosed down in the mud. The bodies were presumed to be inside the vehicle, the Acantha reported.

"Exact location of the tragedy is the mid-west side of the lake, where the inflowing canal is kept open and the waters occasionally are slightly frozen over. About 25 Choteau fishermen were fishing on the same spot last Sunday.

"An Acantha staff member who was among the first to arrive at the scene late yesterday, said a thin coating of oil was on the water. When the oil was splashed away, the car and its white, new Montana license plates were clearly visible some 12 feet below the surface of the water.

"Machinery to hoist the car out of the water and onto the ice today is being sought. The task is a difficult one because heavy equipment cannot be taken on the ice, it is stated. The automobile may be brought out of the lake sometime today, however," the Acantha reported.

A hat and billfold were found floating on the lake and were thought to be owned by Tayfield Becker. "Thus the man may have freed himself from the car, it is believed," the Acantha stated.

Terry Tennant reported the grim news in the Jan. 24, 1946, Acantha that Sam Becker's body was brought to the surface on Jan. 17 and Tayfield Becker's body on Jan. 18, under the supervision of Sheriff Peterson and County Coroner Larry Banks.

"Aided by trucks owned by Choteau people, large logs were hauled to the reservoir and a tripod was erected by sliding two of the large logs across the channel with a block and hoist suspended from the intersection of the tripod.

"When oil and ice had been cleared away, two large hooks were lowered into the water and became affixed to the axle of the car. With the aid of the tripod, the vehicle was raised to the surface.

"Upon examination only one body was found in the car Thursday night, that of Sam Becker. Because of the insufficient height of the tripod, the rescue party was unable to completely extricate the vehicle, which would have facilitated removing the body through the doors.

"Therefore, the rear-vision window was enlarged with an axe and the body recovered through the window. Because of darkness, operations had to be curtailed. Thus, it was necessary to wait for daylight before continuing the search for Tayfield.

"Equipped with Jack Armstrong's truck and winch combined, the rescue party returned to the reservoir Friday morning. After a few unsuccessful tries with a grab nook, Sheriff Peterson was finally able to retrieve Tayfield's body, which had evidently been lying beside the car," the Acantha reported.

Sam Becker was single, and Tayfield Becker had a wife and three children.

Continuing with wintertime tragedies, Roland Birdeau, 45, of Fairfield and sons, Lynn Joseph "Joe," 3, and Larry, 4 and a half, drowned at about 5 p.m. on Jan. 18, 1953, when their car plunged into a nine-foot-deep open channel on Freezout Lake. Area ranchers Frank and Dave Harris rescued a passenger, Carsten Calkins of Butte. Sheriff Peterson and others dragged the channel with grappling hooks before bringing out the last of the bodies before 10 p.m., the Acantha reported.

The news continued, "Calkins held the youngest boy above water for a quarter hour or more before the Harris brothers could reach the scene, but the boy slipped from his grasp and Calkins was barely able to hold on to the line thrown to him. Birdeau missed a line thrown to him and disappeared. More than 100 persons lined the banks as searchers sailed back and forth across the car dragging for the bodies. All three were found near the auto.

"The four apparently were unable to see the open channel. ... Apparently the four were driving on the ice-covered lake seeking a place to fish when the car suddenly plunged into about nine feet of water. Part of the car remained out of the water," the Acantha reported. Birdeau was married and had two other children, a daughter and a 1-year-old son.

On Feb. 18, 1965, the Acantha reported that Mrs. Pearl Allen, 32, of Augusta and William Ish, 75, of Sun River were killed shortly before noon on Feb. 16, when their auto dropped through the ice on Willow Creek Reservoir into 14 feet of water.

Longtime friends and distant relatives, Allen and Ish had left Augusta at 11 a.m. to go ice fishing in the reservoir, seven miles north of Augusta. They drove parallel to the bank about 50 feet from shore. When the car hit a thin spot in the ice, it nosed into the water and disappeared. The sheriff used a winch line hooked onto the vehicle's rear and dragged it to shore. Allen, married, had a son, 11, and daughter, 6. Ish was married and had five daughters, a step-daughter and a son.

And then there are other cases, with no closure. In

October 1940, Grover Cleveland Forgey, 55, a longtime former Choteau resident, drowned in Flathead Lake. He had hooked a fish, lost his balance and fell overboard in a rowboat equipped with a motor. His wife, Frances, fell in, too, but managed to cling to the boat and hail for help. The lake was 300 feet deep and Forgey's body was never recovered.

As ice melts away from the surface of the ponds and reservoirs in the area, the inviting water might be just as dangerous as the thin ice.

A dare proved fatal on June 8, 1956, when a young man drowned in Pishkun Reservoir, 15 miles southwest of Choteau, the Acantha reported.

"Teton County officers last Friday evening dragged the reservoir and canal for the body of Airman 2nd Class Gerald A. Kootz, 19, of the 29th Air Division Headquarters squadron.

"The next morning one of the four airmen who were with the drowned man found Kootz's body in the main irrigation canal. He had drowned while attempting to swim the canal. He and the four companions had been camping near the mouth of Sun River Canyon.

"Teton County Sheriff T.J. Dellwo, who directed the all-night search, [using a 100-foot-long net] said Kootz and another airman dared each other to swim across the canal fully clothed. The other youth had reached the opposite shore when he heard Kootz scream for help. He plunged into the canal, but Kootz disappeared before he could reach him.

"Dellwo said it was this same airman who found the body by wading down the canal in three feet of water after Fairfield [Greenfields] irrigation project officials shut off the flow of water from the Diversion Dam on the Sun River," the Acantha explained.

In July 1962, 11-year-old Jay Leslie Luinstra drowned on a Friday afternoon when he fell from a raft into a gravel pit pond near the location of the former Choteau city dump.

The youngster and his brother both slipped off the raft into the pond, which in places was about seven feet deep, the Acantha reported. The youngsters had been fishing in Spring Creek and reportedly wandered to the pond and raft.

The brother swam to shore and ran home, told his mother, who then rushed to the pond and pulled the unconscious youngster to shore. She called her brother, Elmer Baker, and they attempted artificial respiration without success, according to Larry Banks, county coroner, the Acantha reported.

The drowning was the first in Teton County that year, but not the last.

In September, Donald David Walker of Black Eagle drowned at Eureka Lake, nine miles northwest of Choteau.

Walker and a friend were skin diving and taking turns with scuba gear when Walker swam from shore to a raft in the middle of the lake. The friend noticed Walker had not surfaced. He borrowed retired Choteau baker Ray McClue's boat and rowed to the raft and pulled the dead youth from beneath it. Dr. L.S. Crary, a local doctor and dentist, was already fishing at Eureka and helped with getting the body from the raft to the shore. Walker was pronounced dead at the Teton Memorial Hospital.

Lastly, a local tragedy that remains in many memories occurred on July 11, 1965, when standout Choteau High School athlete Dennis Paul Rice, 16, drowned in Bynum Reservoir.

About 8:30 p.m. he attempted to swim from a raft anchored off the reservoir's northeast shore near the east end of the dike. Four other teenagers had been on the raft. Rice was 25 to 35 feet from the raft when he flailed the water and disappeared from sight, the Acantha reported.

The men had been on family picnics at the reservoir and

had pushed the raft into the water and anchored it about 100 yards from shore in 12 feet of water. They were too far away to save their friend, having left the raft first. They hailed two fishermen who helped search the area for about 45 minutes before discovering the body.

Rice attended elementary school at Bynum and would have been a Choteau high school senior in September 1965. He also would have attended the American Legion-sponsored Boys State in August. An outstanding football player, he was one of three Choteau High School football players to be named to an All-Conference Northern Division grid team in December 1964.

Rice was active in many school activities and hoped to gain a West Point appointment when he graduated from high school. At the May 1965 "Class Night," now known as the Awards Night, Rice was listed as a student council officer, a third-year pep band rear guard and a football letterman. He also was a cast member of the junior class play.

His photo as a Boys State delegate appeared on the Acantha's front page on May 27, 1965, but then his class photo appeared on the front page outlining the tragic circumstances on July 15, 1965.

The community was shocked and saddened and it was with a heavy heart that football coach John Rose presented the first Dennis Rice Memorial Award plaque to his parents, Leonard and Mabel Rice, at the Class Night in May 1966.

Thereafter, the Dennis Rice Award was given each year to the outstanding male senior athlete starting with Dennis Van Auken in 1967 and ending with Halvor Kamrud in 1988.

Published in the Choteau Acantha Jan. 27, and Feb. 3, 10, 2016.

The North Carolina Man

1923

The commotion at Klick's tourist camp shocked the denizens in the Sun River Canyon country west of Augusta and made front-page news on June 28, 1923.

The Choteau Acantha and its competing newspaper, the Choteau Montanan, republished portions of a Great Falls newspaper report.

"Alleged bank thief captured in Sun River Canyon. John D. Sykes Jr., [age 28] former teller of the [First & Citizens] National Bank of Elizabeth City, North Carolina, and indicted on the charge that he violated the national banking laws in connection with the theft of $26,000 from his bank last September, was overpowered and arrested early Tuesday morning [June 26] by local and federal officers as he entered Klick's tourist camp unarmed, seven miles from his fortified cabin in the Sun River Canyon wilderness. Sykes, who is a prisoner in the Great Falls city jail, is a member of an old Southern family and has been the object of a nationwide search since his disappearance nine months ago, officers said.

"Sykes' capture was accomplished by Ray S. Gaunt, police lieutenant, who was delegated to the work by Chief Marcus Anderson and a special agent of the Department of Justice and two representatives of bond houses interested in the North Carolina bank. Warned that Sykes was desperate, the officers went into the mountains in the guise of fishermen on a holiday, hoping to find an opportunity to make the arrest without gunplay. They stopped at the Klick camp, seven miles from the Sykes cabin, and while eating a belated supper, they recognized Sykes when he walked into the room.

"Leaps upon Sykes. To avoid exposing women tourists [including the Misses Evelyn Hansen, Phyllis Green and Beth Cleland of Choteau] who were in the room to probable shooting, the officers waited until the last of the women had left, chatting at times with the affable Sykes. Gaunt then maneuvered until he was close to Sykes, leaped upon him and bore him backwards. With the assistance of the other officers, Gaunt handcuffed Sykes, after a sharp battle.

"'You are under arrest,' said Gaunt to the prisoner. 'Do you know why?'

"Sykes paused a moment before he decided to yield and then answered, 'Yes.'

"Sykes' first question was about his mother. He had not heard from his people since leaving Elizabeth City last September. His parents, according to the officers, are not wealthy, but are of old Southern stock and are held in high regard in their home community. The son served in the navy during the war and had been in the Elizabeth City bank for three years at the time of his disappearance.

"At the Klick camp the officers were told that Sykes kept 16 guns in his cabin, as well as a large supply of ammunition and more than $500 worth of provisions. The log walls of the cabin made the building a veritable fortress and Sykes could have withstood a long siege before surrendering. When he first located in the mountains he always went armed, but quit carrying a revolver when he learned that it was in violation of forest regulations.

"Is Haughty Here. After Sykes's arrival at the Great Falls jail he haughtily declined to talk to reporters, but the officers quote him as admitting his identity and the accuracy of the North Carolina charges. He told them of his flight from North Carolina, his arrival in Great Falls, his mountain cabin and his hopes of avoiding discovery in the Sun River Canyon, they say. The Sykes cabin is in one of the most inaccessible places in the Montana Rockies. ...

"Extremely Popular. As W.D. 'Dave' Simpson [an alias] Sykes made no effort to avoid his few neighbors and his friendliness and generosity caused him to become extremely popular. Those who knew him best were very strong in his defense after his arrest and during the fight with the officers one mountaineer started to interfere in Sykes's behalf, but desisted when he saw the officers' badges."

After embezzlement suspect Sykes, alias Simpson, was captured, the local newspapers told of his coming to Montana.

The Acantha republished a report from the Great Falls Tribune, "According to the account of Sykes's previous history given the officers, the banker was highly respected in his home community. The officers quote him as saying that he took the first money from his bank to gamble with, intimating that he lost more than $5,000 on horse races. Realizing that he could never make good this amount, and that detection was inevitable, he, on Sept. 3, 1922, took enough additional cash to start with somewhere else and fled. He declared that he could have taken three times as much money had he been disposed to do so.

"From Elizabeth City, North Carolina, Sykes went to Chicago, and remained there but a day or two, coming from Chicago direct to Great Falls. Here he learned about the inaccessibility of the Sun River Canyon country and decided to locate there. He purchased a cabin from Bruce Neal, Augusta game warden, and planned to begin raising silver black fox for the market. ...

"Had one man gone into the canyon alone to arrest

Sykes, he never would have been captured without shoot-ing, officers declared. He told the officers while on the way to the Falls that he was glad that he had not been armed.

"'If I had been armed, I surely would have made you kill me,' he told them, they declare.

"Sykes's attitude of desperation caused the officers to keep him under handcuffs throughout the long night trip to Great Falls, and to take precautions against any attempt at suicide. Coming out of the canyon, the road follows a cliff with a sheer drop of 500 feet at many places, and the pris-oner was carefully guarded while it was possible for him to leap over the precipice. He showed no loss of nerve ex-cept when he asked about his mother. Tears then streamed down his face."

The Independent newspaper in Elizabeth City had re-ported on the theft nine months earlier, "Sells birthright for a remnant of calico. Elizabeth City boy robs First & Cit-izens National Bank of nearly $25,000 by quick work and is missing. John D. Sykes Jr. for three years a trusted em-ployee of the First & Citizens National Bank of this city and half owner of the finest poultry farm in Pasquotank Coun-ty, wrecked his home, sacrificed his future and made a com-plete mess of his life by stealing around $25,000 from the bank in which he was employed and becoming a fugitive from justice.

"The fact of young Sykes' defalcation and disappearance was made known only this week. He left town on Sunday, Sept. 3, 1922. A careful audit of every department of the bank this week, with only a few minor items yet to trace, discloses a shortage in Sykes' accounts, which will come close to $25,000, which is the amount of his bond.

"Sykes, like all the other employees of the bank, was under a $25,000 bond of the Fidelity Trust & Deposit Co. of Baltimore. The bonding company has set in motion, machinery which has detective agencies and the police of many cities on the trail of the fugitive.

"The young defaulter is the son of John D. Sykes Sr., manager of the local office of the Western Union Telegraph Co. of this city. His father and mother are two of the most honorable, hard-working and highly respected citizens of the community. They had made many sacrifices for the boy and after he had begun to make good in the bank. They helped him to establish a poultry business on their little farm near the outskirts of the city and the Sykes Poultry Farm had already become one of the show places of the county. But the boy got another thing in his head and went to hell before his family, employees and friends knew which way he was heading."

Sykes, 28, waived extradition and was transported to North Carolina where he posted $10,000 bail (money raised by members of the local First Baptist Church) and waited for his court date in October. In the meantime, the local newspaper, the Independent, explained what had happened to the "young boy" who supposedly had been led astray by a married woman with a police record.

Sykes made away with $25,825.94 ($386,300 in today's dollars) before he left town on Sept. 3, 1922.

After an honorable discharge from the navy, Sykes started work as a collection teller and savings clerk at the First & Citizens National Bank in Elizabeth City in August 1919. He was able to abscond with money, including receipts from Christmas savings accounts hidden in his own safety deposit box, between scheduled audits, the window being Aug. 15 to the day after Labor Day. He took the money, went to Norfolk, Virginia, where he bought a train ticket to Columbus, Ohio.

After that, he bought a train ticket to Chicago. There he exchanged the money for thousand dollar bills, two or three at each bank. That took about two days. He also bought a diamond, some guns and some fishing tackle.

Then he bought a ticket to Great Falls. "I read an article in the Field and Stream about Troy, Montana, being a good place to hunt and fish and as Troy was a small place and I doubted if I could get what things I needed, I looked up Great Falls. On the train I met a man who told me about the country around Sun River Canyon and I decided to go there," he told a reporter. He stayed at the Johnson Hotel in Great Falls when he arrived on Sept 10.

There he met his girlfriend, Mrs. Adelaide Penelope Lyons, 22, who he had sent for by telegram from Chicago.

He put some money in the banks in Great Falls, and carried the balance of it with him when they went to Augusta. He spent a week in getting a place in the mountains to live.

They went to Hoxey's cabin in the canyon that he rented from Sept. 23, 1922, to March 24, 1923. Then he bought Montana Deputy Game Warden Bruce Neal's cabin in the canyon for $4,000 with checks drawn on the Great Falls National Bank. Neal had set the price and said that was as cheap as he could sell it.

With the cabin came a few chickens, five horses, one colt, two mowers and a few farming implements, he said. "I entered into an agreement with the Great Falls Silver Fox Farm for the purchase of two pair of breeding foxes on which agreement I paid $500 down, under date of March 9, and upon delivery on Oct. 15, I was to pay $4,500 more," he said.

He loaned Leo Klick $500, but after his arrest he signed over Klick's note to the bonding company. Klick owed him $44 which he repaid by check on the Westside State Bank of Great Falls, and which Sykes also endorsed to the bond company.

"It was my intention to start a ranch and fox farm to

get in a position whereby I could make restitution," he said. Was his girlfriend an accomplice, the reporter asked. "No," he said, "Just before my alleged wife, Mrs. Penelope Lyons, went home about two weeks ago, I told her everything concerning the transactions at the bank. I bought her a diamond ring, worth $230, from Crown Jewelry in Great Falls," Sykes said. Lyons said they were planning on getting married after she divorced her husband.

As the alleged embezzler waited for his court date in the fall of 1923, the press reported on how his companion, Penelope Lyons, broke down and gave law enforcement Sykes's location in the remote Sun River Canyon country.

"The defalcation of young Sykes is a dramatic chapter in the life of the town," the Independent wrote. Sykes was a trusted promising employee, the pride of his parents, who was "generally regarded as a man of sober habits, industry and thrift," it opined.

"But he became infatuated with a young grass widow by the name of Penelope Lyons. Following a hot and furious courtship with Mrs. Lyons in the summer of 1922, young Sykes left the city on Sept. 3. Mrs. Lyons left the city for parts unknown about the same time," the news said.

A $1,000 reward was offered for Sykes's capture and his picture was posted in banks and post offices all over the country. "But he covered his tracks well and might have been at liberty yet, but for the woman in the case."

Sykes had not disposed of all of the money ($25,895.94) with which he got away. When caught, he turned the balance over to the officers. "It is believed he will plead guilty, and throw himself on the mercy of the court," the news offered.

Lyons had spent the previous nine months with Sykes in the remote cabin on the South Fork of the Sun River, but in June Sykes asked her to go back to see how things were going in his old home town and to get news of his mother.

"She had not been many days in town before officers of the Department of Justice had taken her into custody and put her through the third degree. Even under the grueling inquisition she refused to tell the whereabouts of her friend. She swore she would die before she would tell. Finally under continued pressure, she said she would tell with the consent of the boy's mother."

The mother begged Lyons to tell all she knew because she wanted her son to pay the penalty and begin life anew, the news reported. Likewise, Sykes's father had faith in "the boy," and believed that his son was the victim of evil influences, and that he would "make restitution when he comes to his senses. ... 'My boy is pure gold..'" the news reported the father saying.

Lyons was assured by law enforcement that she would not be prosecuted and that she would receive the reward if she told what she knew.

"She said she first met Sykes through a flirtation in the moving picture theater and afterwards saw him as many as three times a week."

The Independent reported that Lyons was separated from her husband, Henry, who she had married five years before. She garnered a police record when she figured in a case in Elizabeth City Police Court, charged with disorderly conduct with two prominent young Elizabeth City men. Henry Lyons divorced Penelope in August 1924.

Sykes pleaded guilty, and community members asked for leniency. He was sentenced to serve a term of from one to three years in the federal penitentiary at Atlanta, Georgia. He married a woman named Mary Owens after he got out of jail and died in 1970 in his hometown.

In January 1924, Lyons sued the bonding company for $2,700 with interest from July 1923, which included the reward and 10 percent of the money recovered. The bonding company refused, alleging, "She had knowledge of Sykes's whereabouts; she went and lived with him in the cabin in Montana, and she was a participant in the crime and an accessory before the fact. To give her any money would be inequitable and unconscionable."

It claimed that she was never promised the reward, and that it belonged rightfully to Ray Gaunt, a Great Falls police officer who effected Sykes's capture. Lyons claimed she had nothing to do with the crime, "but she doesn't explain the fact that she went to Montana, posed as his wife, shared the money with him and lived on the fat of the land until she was surfeited with luxury such as she had never been favored with in her career, and, gorged with her high living, came back to her mother's little home in the mill district," the Independent wrote. "Like many another woman with a police court record, Penelope probably is a gold digger," the newspaper concluded.

The news reported that letters from Sykes to former acquaintances in the Sun River country told of his imprisonment and payment of the reward to the woman. After receiving it, she left for parts unknown. ▨

Published in the Choteau Acantha Aug. 14, 21, 28, Sept. 4, 2019.

— 15 —
Abandoned horses
1926

Among the 241 laws approved by the state Legislature in the spring of 1925, was one authorizing county commissioners to order roundups of abandoned "worthless" range horses and providing for their sale or slaughter.

It took a year for some Teton County residents to take advantage of the law. In April 1926 the Acantha reported that some residents of the Greenfields Bench, near Fairfield, petitioned to create a roundup district to include seven townships and a roundup foreman "as a step toward ridding that section of 'abandoned' horses."

The proposed district members could round up and dispose of by sale or otherwise, both branded and unbranded horses deemed as abandoned and public nuisances.

The roundup district included land south and east of Choteau and south of the Great Northern Railway right-of-way between Choteau and Power. It was "designed to rid that portion of the county of 'Cayuses' that are eating their heads off on range that might be used more profitably," the Acantha reported.

The May 13 legal notice advised that beginning on or within 10 days after June 12, 1926, a roundup of abandoned horses would be held. It described the district boundaries, which were more extensive that previously discussed, and ended with "and all abandoned horses taken up in such roundup and not lawfully reclaimed by the owner, will be sold or otherwise disposed of."

Foreman C.W. Burns set up his headquarters at Choteau. By then, 35 stockowners and taxpayers had signed the petition and they guaranteed they would pay the roundup expenses, although it was expected to be a self supporting enterprise through receipts placed in the "abandoned horse fund."

Abandoned horses were defined as "any horses, mare, gelding, filly, jack, mule or any other animal of the genus Equus, of the age of one year or over and unbranded or, if branded, which escaped assessment for taxation for the year next preceding its impounding, and running at large on the open range." It included foals running with dams. An animal not bearing a decipherable brand as recorded in the office of the recorder of marks and brands, "shall be deemed unbranded."

Open range was defined as "all lands not enclosed by a legal fence and all highways outside of private enclosures, when used by the public, whether formally dedicated to public use or not."

After advertising the sale for 10 days, owners could reclaim by purchase. There were a few other details regarding how to deal with ownership disputes and the receipts.

The first sale was on July 12 at the Great Northern stockyards in Choteau. The ad listed every horse by color, sex, age, weight and brand, if known, all 600 of them that had been gathered over eight days.

Auctioneer E.D. Forrest had an easy job because he sold every animal to George Lyman for the Butte Packing Co. at a straight price of $3.50 per head. The final accounting was $1,590.50 in receipts and $1,386.94 in expenses leaving a balance of $203.56 in the abandoned horse fund until Nov. 30, when the money would be transferred to the county's general fund.

The expenses included payments for Burns's salary and

wages to riders, herders, the auctioneer and a cook, the rent of pasture and corrals and the legal notice.

Burns and Martin Rose, with the cooperation of ranchers and their riders, were trailed out of town for Butte the following Tuesday by Lyman and his riders, Burns and Rose traveling with the cavalcade to the Lewis and Clark County line. "Burns said this morning that the purpose of the law was to rid the range of the horses and that the only way one could get enough out of the bunch to pay expenses and avoid an assessment against the roundup petitioners, was to sell the good ones with the scrubs, getting rid of the animals as soon as possible and cutting the expense of holding the horses which ran into $75 a day after they were brought to Choteau," the Acantha reported.

Fast forward to February 2009, when state Rep. Russell Bean, writing a column in the Acantha, said a bill had been introduced to allow equine processing plants in Montana because of the problem of abandoned horses. "Since the last horse slaughterhouse in the country closed, people [want] nothing to do with horses they can't keep anymore, so they just abandon them," Bean wrote. The bill didn't pass. ▟

Published in the Choteau Acantha March 15, 2017.

— 16 —

Blackface Minstrel Shows Once Commonplace

1926-1954

Blackface minstrel shows were a popular form of American entertainment starting in the post-Civil War era and they persisted as entertaining fundraisers for some Choteau area organizations from the 1920s to about 1954.

With the Black Lives Matter movement raising awareness of systemic and institutionalized racism in America, this tale looks at how these patently offensive shows were once considered wholesome entertainment in rural Montana and other places.

The portrayal of negative stereotypes of Blacks has declined with the civil rights movement, and while mocking people of color is disrespectful and unacceptable behavior, this article serves as a reminder of how far the United States has come in addressing racism and how far it has yet to go.

Readers are advised that the following tale contains racist and offensive language.

In December 1924 the Acantha reported that the Choteau Woman's Club library fund was richer by more than $200 as a result of the "splendid turnout" at the high school auditorium for a home talent minstrel show, staged under the direction of Hugh Wypper. "It is planned, according to Mrs. R. E. Nelson of the Woman's Club committee, to make the minstrel an annual affair."

The following spring a minstrel troupe, made up of local

talent from Choteau, traveled to Dutton on invitation of the Dutton Masonic lodge, "to present a blackface program for Dutton masons and their guests."

The Acantha reported in April 1925, "The local blackface minstrel company, organized primarily for a Woman's Club benefit entertainment given last fall, disbanded last Saturday night after having played three engagements in addition to its first. The troupe has been under the management of Hugh Wypper who authorizes the announcement that further engagements during the present season will not be considered as the supply of cocoa butter is running low like the stock of gags. Members will take the summer off to rest their faces."

In March 1926 a minstrel troupe from Dutton was the feature attraction when 220 masons, eastern stars and partners of the Dutton and Choteau lodges gathered at the Masonic lodge rooms in Choteau.

Wypper organized the blackface "Teton minstrels" in December 1926 that played benefits for the Ladies' Aid of the Community Church in Fairfield, and at Dutton for the Boy Scouts.

In February 1928 the Acantha promoted a home talent minstrel show as an "annual song fest of cottonland folks" to be held at the auditorium in Choteau, complete with "old time plantation melodies, latest hits, jokes, quartets and instrumentals to make the evening happy."

The annual Negro minstrel by the men of Choteau was "so popular and scored such a hit that it was the talk of the country for miles around."

The opening number that February was an ensemble entitled, "In the Land of Cotton," and contained snatches from 10 of the most famous old time plantation airs and melodies, including, "Since Lizzie Changed Her Name to Baby Lincoln," "Red Lips Kiss My Blues Away" and

"Swanee River."

At the annual Farmers' Fun Feed in March 1934, the main features of the program were musical numbers, stunts, one-act plays and a blackface skit put on by the Bynum community.

At the fun feed in March 1936, with the skit, "A Dark Affair," the Fairfield community representatives took to the stage. "The women were all dolled up as darkies and they had a line of songs and jokes that were popular."

In March 1938, for the benefit of the civic fund, the Choteau Lions Club presented an all male blackface minstrel show at the high school auditorium. "The show was divided into three parts, a Negro spiritual meeting, with a Negro preacher officiating and the congregation rendering the good old spiritual songs interspersed with Glory hallelujahs; a celebration of the Negro workers on the plantation at the close of the cotton-picking season; and a skit entitled, "The Mudpuddle County Court Case."

More talent shows and even the educational conference, the Chautauqua, included blackface skits in the 1930s and 1940s.

The apparent last reference to the now-offensive term was a display ad in April 1954, for a bandanna minstrel show, sponsored by the American Legion of Brady in the Brady gym with a chorus of 40 junior high students, dancing acts, jokes and laughs, plus a skit, "The Shooting of Dan McGrew." "This is the first time that this has ever been done in 'blackface' to the best of anyone's knowledge," the ad read.

After that, the term "blackface" seems to have been reserved for ewes and rams.

Published in the Choteau Acantha July 29, 2020.

Farm Bureau Fun Feeds

1926-1949

The Teton County Farm Bureau's annual Fun Feed was a farmers-only event in the high school gymnasium in Choteau each spring that drew 500 people.

County Agent Robert Clarkson originated the fun feed, although the first one, on Feb. 5, 1926, wasn't called that. It included a luncheon at 50 cents per plate with a speaker, and entertainment provided by the high school orchestra, the glee club and community singing.

Communities represented were Dutton, Farmington, Fairfield, Bynum, Bole, Power, Agawam, Choteau, Pendroy and Collins.

After the second annual Farm Bureau Fun Feed drew 300 people, the Acantha remarked, "Never before have so many been seated at one time at any farm event." Farm Bureau President L.G. Passmore of Farmington introduced the speaker whose subject was sugar beets.

After hosting a "heavy" speaker in the 1928 event, the fourth Fun Feed in March 1929 drew 530 people to what was billed as, "this time nothing heavy." The menu was roast pork and applesauce, baked potatoes, creamed peas, cabbage slaw and celery with blueberry pie for dessert and coffee. The fixings included 230 pounds of pork, 1,320 buns, 115 pies, 250 pounds of potatoes and a case of celery.

The Acantha gave the 1930 Fun Feed an extensive write-up. "Teton County's fifth annual Fun Feed — the like of which there is not another in the state — was held here

Thursday night. It was in fact what it is in name, an evening of riotous and untrammeled fun, plus a monstrous feed, for which covers were laid for 550, but the actual number fed was considerably in excess of that number."

Clarkson and Choteau Lions Club President Jas. Eckford played a trick on the crowd by pretending that the event was being broadcast live on KFBB radio. The chief station announcer and station executives were in on the joke.

"As is the custom, the various communities gave their songs and yells, and the rivalry was keen and the results uncommonly good."

The after-dinner program, a hog-calling contest, was announced with contestants: Emil Depner, Farmington; A.L. Meyers, Fairfield; J.W. Moore, Bynum; W.D. Dauwalder, Bole; H.S. Hodges, Dutton; Matt Decker, Power; J.H. Van Auken, Agawam; H.L. Stafford, Choteau; Paul Rice, Pendroy; and E.R. McLean of Collins.

Depner won a young pig as first prize and Hodges came in second, getting 25 baby chicks donated by a Lewistown hatchery.

Vilate Stott of Bynum won the chicken-calling contest for women, and second place went to Mrs. Fred Woodward of Agawam. The contestants were Mrs. E.R. McLean, Collins; Mrs. Paul Mathis, Bole; Mrs. John Mathison, Dutton; Mrs. L.S. Baldwin, Fairfield; Woodward; Mrs. J.E. Hodgskiss, Choteau; Stott and Mrs. John Carlson, Farmington. The winner was offered her choice between a purse and 25 baby chicks. Stott chose the chicks, and the purse went to Woodward.

A pillow race followed the chicken-calling contest with eight on each team, the members from each community. "The contest was a hot one and the women nosed out ahead of the men by a few seconds. A small box of candy was awarded to each woman on the team, and a small box of cigars to each man," the Acantha reported. A dance was held after that.

KFBB radio broadcast the 1931 Fun Feed. By then the Depression was taking its toll on personal finances and Clarkson cancelled the event set for March 1932, but he organized a low-key, no-banquet event in November with a good program "to drive dull care away."

The Fun Feed was cancelled again in 1933, but the crowds were back in March 1934 and the event was held each year with each successive one being touted as "best in recent years," "most successful ever" and "best ever."

The Fun Feeds continued during World War II until the proposed 20th annual one in March 1945 was postponed "until war conditions are more favorable.

"The group expressed a desire to cooperate with the recent order for closing amusement places at midnight, and also took into consideration the acute conditions prevailing at this time in the matter of food and gasoline rationing."

The last one occurred in March 1949, and in January 1953, the Acantha editor wrote, "The Fun Feed, which was quite the thing some years back, has fallen by the wayside since there hasn't been a place large enough to take care of it." A push to turn the old grade school into a civic center to house it never materialized.

Published in the Choteau Acantha March 1, 2017.

— 18 —
Gibson Dam
1926

The headline in one local newspaper in May 1926, that read, "Favorable to Gibson Dam," brought long-awaited news to the water users in the vicinity of Fairfield and Fort Shaw.

"A favorable report on the proposed Gibson Dam site in the Sun River irrigation project in Montana, by Pres. C.H. Clap of the University of Montana, was made public Tuesday by the Bureau of Reclamation. The report says that conditions are entirely suitable for the construction of a high arch dam 175 feet in height. [The height is now listed as 199 feet.] The Reclamation Bureau is planning to start construction work on the project at an early date," the May 26 River Press stated.

A few details had to be worked out first. Sixty percent of the landowners in the Greenfields Irrigation District had to sign the bureau's contract: the government would finish the project and the district would pay the money back on the basis of 5 percent of the average crop value, the Acantha reported.

In other words, if the average production on the district was $30 per acre per year, the repayment obligation would be $1.50 per year per irrigable acre.

In July 1926, Teton County District Judge J. Greene confirmed the proceedings of the Greenfields commissioners in reference to district organization and the execution of the "Beaver Creek Dam" contract.

At some point after the project was envisioned to build a dam at the mouth of Beaver Creek west of Augusta, the name of the proposed dam was changed to Gibson, presumably for Paris Gibson, the founder of Great Falls, but the Acantha never mentioned how that happened.

"The contract was awarded at Washington during the past week by Secretary of the Interior Hubert Work to the Utah Construction Co. of Ogden, Utah, whose bid of $1,566,240, was the lowest of seven submitted. This is considerably below the estimates of the engineers of the Bureau of Reclamation.

"Some preliminary work will be done this winter, and it is expected that active construction will be underway in the early spring," the Sept. 23 Big Timber Pioneer announced.

The Sept. 23, 1926, Acantha gave the details. "George O. Sanford, manager of the Sun River project was notified by telegraph yesterday that the Department of the Interior has approved the bid of the Utah Construction Co. for the construction of the storage reservoir at Beaver Creek. ...

"The contract will be signed by the Secretary of the Interior and forwarded to the company by the chief engineer of the Reclamation Bureau within a short time, Sanford said. Notice that the bid has been approved permits the contractors to immediately start preparations for the work. One of the first items will be reconstruction of the Sun River Canyon road between Diversion Dam camp and Beaver Creek. Improvements on the road between the canyon and Augusta also will be necessary before the heavy equipment, reinforcing steel and cement can be freighted to the site."

Reporting on the water users' celebration in Fairfield on Sept. 18, the Acantha stated, "The celebration has been long looked forward to by the settlers of the project and with it is ended a fight of 15 years or more to secure the reservoir. It is to be completed in three years and in addition to furnishing additional and often much needed water for the 40,000 acres or so now under the ditch, it will make possible the extension of laterals to supply between 40,000 and 50,000 acres more irrigable land.

"The program started at 3 p.m. with addresses by T.J. Walsh, senior U.S. senator from Montana, and Scott Leavitt, representative in Congress from the Second District. The chairman of the meeting was Sam Ness, secretary of the Greenfields Irrigation District. A baseball game between Fairfield and Cascade followed the program and in the evening a dance was held in the large community hall. Probably 400 people from Augusta, Fairfield, Choteau, Great Falls and Helena were at the afternoon meeting. The ladies of the Fairfield Lutheran Church served lunch from noon until 9 in the evening and the supper at the carnival dance was provided by the Ladies' Aid of the community church.

"Sen. T.J. Walsh, first on the program, praised the Utah Construction Co., successful bidders for the dam contract, and predicted that the Fairfield section is destined to become one of the most densely settled regions of Montana," the Acantha reported.

Leavitt "spoke of the recently enacted law erasing more than two million dollars of indebtedness on the four federal projects in Montana as the most important act of the last session of Congress, characterizing it as 'a new declaration of independence for the reclamation projects of the west.' He paid compliment to the other members of the Montana delegation in both houses of Congress, saying the matter was worked out with the complete cooperation of all.

"Referring to his frequent visits to the project in the past, Leavitt said: 'You told me that the greatest need of the project is this dam.' He joined Sen. Walsh in expressing pleasure that recent developments made possible a gathering to celebrate the consummation of a contract to make this hope of years a reality.

"Scores of people from Choteau motored to Fairfield for the program last Saturday afternoon and more still to be at the big dance at the community hall which held a throng from all over this section from early Saturday evening until well along towards morning," the Acantha stated.

In July 2019 Gibson Dam on the Sun River west of Augusta marked its 90th year since it was constructed.

The whole building project, pegged at $3 million, (including $1,566,240 to be paid to the Utah Construction Co.) started in September 1926 with the necessary survey for laying out the camp after which the machinery began arriving in the canyon. The project was to take three years.

The first report noted that Utah Construction Co. officials, Warren Wattis, treasurer; Paul Wattis, assistant superintendent; and B. Boulger, chief clerk, visited the dam site. A.E. Paddock was set to remain on the ground in charge of the work, making his headquarters in Great Falls for the winter.

"The Utah company representatives recently closed a deal with the Montana Power Co. for the furnishing of such electricity as might be used on the contract in the way of lighting, power and the like, and work will be started at once by the power company to lay poles and wires to the dam site.

"The company furnished the government power to the building of the Sun River [diversion] dam, and the wires run to that place, within four or five miles of the Gibson Dam, and over a good road, so that the job of getting electricity on the grounds will not be a heavy one. As many as 500 men will be used at various times during progress of the work," the Acantha reported.

Lewis and Clark National Forest officials also had work to do. Forest Deputy Supervisor A. Duncan Moir announced that the agency would have to rebuild its Sun River Canyon telephone line, because of construction work on the new dam's electric power line.

In October 1926, Dr. George E. Keller of Choteau reported that he and Dr. Gray made their first professional trip to the Sun River Canyon as physicians for the construction crew engaged in preliminary work on the new "Beaver Creek" dam.

"Dr. Keller says that quite a city is springing up near the dam site, where it is expected between 300 and 500 men will be employed next summer. New buildings included bunkhouses and mess halls and a bungalow or two for officials. Work on widening the canyon road is to start next week, according to the local man."

John L. Savage of Denver, the federal reclamation engineer who designed Gibson Dam, arrived in October to confer with Paddock after which construction proceeded in earnest.

The first work, according to the Mineral Independent newspaper, was to build the camp buildings, including an office and houses, a short distance away. Road improvements included gravel on the road between Augusta and the Diversion Dam at a number of points and material improvements on the few miles of highway between the diversion and Gibson.

The next phase would employ 75 to 100 men to bore a tunnel, which would serve as a spillway for the dam. "None of the flood waters of the Sun River will go over the top of the new dam, according to [Denver-based dam engineer] J.L. Savage's plans, but will be carried off by a tunnel which will have its exit under the concrete structure."

The construction news during November and December included a destructive brushfire, a legal dispute regarding the Ralph Allan dude ranch and the project's first fatality.

By 1925 the Augusta area was the base for several dude ranches, including the Allan ranch in the canyon, Big George Basin Ranch and Sun River Camp west of Augusta, and the Stecker ranch near Gilman.

Besides the Allan ranch, the backed-up water behind Gibson Dam would affect some campgrounds.

The U.S. Forest Service had developed several campgrounds in the canyon four years earlier in May 1921, according to the Acantha.

The first campsite was about one mile up from Diversion Dam, the second near Beaver Creek and one or two others in the main canyon. Each camp was provided with a stone fireplace and holes in which to bury garbage. They were located where they were easily accessible by automobile and in the immediate vicinity of good trout fishing streams.

"Medicine Hot Springs, which have been famous for hundreds of years to the Indians and to white people since the expedition of Lewis and Clark, will be cleared of all rubbish and underbrush near the springs by the forest guides and nearby residents and will be kept clean for the use of people this summer," the Acantha reported in 1921.

"The Forest Service is requiring all campers to camp at least 50 rods from the springs so that the springs will be a clean, neat place for bathing instead of the usual display of empty tin cans, bottles, broken boxes and other rubbish. The Indians even yet camp quite frequently near these springs during the winter and spring months. The old Indian legend has it that bathing in these springs will cure all ills, hence the name, Medicine Hot Springs. All campsites will be ready for use by July 1.

"The road to and above Allan's ranch will probably be repaired by the Forest Service so as to be accessible by auto. The first campsite will be four miles west of Allan's ranch and tourists may motor as far as this ranch by auto but will have to either walk the remaining four miles or travel by horseback.

"Several disastrous fires have been caused in the Sun River Canyon through the thoughtlessness of campers and the Forest Service is urging everyone, campers, tourists and autoists to be careful with all fires, lighted cigarettes, cigar stubs and matches while in the forest," the newspaper stated in 1921.

After work on the proposed dam began in the fall of 1926, construction workers let a destructive brush fire get out of control. A month later, the government condemned the Allan ranch when the owners refused an offer of $10,000, ($142,000 in today's dollars) and flying rocks from a dynamite explosion set off by a road crew killed a fellow worker.

With hundreds of construction workers expected in the canyon and the surrounding national forest, the U.S. Forest Service cast a wary eye to the buildup. It wasn't long before their fears were confirmed.

On Nov. 18, 1926, the Acantha reported that the "Utah Construction Co. men let brush fires get out of control. Forest Service to push charge."

The article was short. "A forest fire, started from brush fires which were allowed to get out of control by employees of the Utah Construction Co., holder of the contract for the new Beaver Creek [Gibson] dam, burned over five acres of second growth timber on Norwegian Gulch, midway between the mouth of Beaver Creek and Home Gulch, in Sun River Canyon, Sunday evening, according to a report by Deputy Supervisor A.D. Moir of the Lewis and Clark Forest. Moir said Tuesday that no arrests had yet been made but that the Forest Service expects to press charges against the construction company.

"Moir stated that the fire is particularly deplorable in

that it practically ruined one of the few camping spots that will remain below Beaver Creek after the completion of the big dam. The Forest Service had recently prepared a public campground just across the road toward Sun River from the acreage which Sunday night's blaze swept."

It wasn't until a month after the dam was finished three years later that the Forest Service contemplated new campgrounds in the vicinity. There was no news about any charges being filed and in December William E. Lockhart succeeded E.H. Myrick as the Lewis and Clark National Forest supervisor.

Charges of a deadly sort, however, took the life of a dam worker, the first of several fatalities to occur before the dam was completed.

On Dec. 9, the Acantha reported, "Death took its first toll from the ranks of workers on the Gibson Dam project in Sun River Canyon, Tuesday night, when L.G. Miller, an employee of the Utah Construction Co. contractors, succumbed at the Gray hospital here [Choteau] to injuries received Monday afternoon when he was struck by flying rocks, thrown by the explosion of a charge of dynamite, set off by a road crew.

"Miller's skull was badly crushed and the severing of an artery in his temple had almost brought death from loss of blood before medical aid could reach him, according to Dr. A.B. Gray of Choteau, company physician, who was summoned Monday by company officials, and who brought the accident victim to his hospital here after rendering first aid. Miller did not regain consciousness, Dr. Gray said, and life was so near extinct when the patient reached the hospital that there was no hope for him.

"Little was known of Miller at the construction company's camp, according to Dr. Gray, excepting that he was thought to have come to Montana from American Falls,

Idaho. He was about 65 years old, and was employed on roadwork in the canyon where the contractors are widening the road from the mouth of the canyon to the dam site.

"No decision as to the disposition of the body which is at the Connor undertaking rooms here, had been made last night, pending the receipt of word from the Utah Construction Co. superintendent, A.A. Paddock, who was at Helena, and who was expected to arrive yesterday in Great Falls, where an effort was being made to get in touch with him. Nothing was known at the camp of Miller's relatives."

This was the first serious accident at the canyon, Dr. Gray said. The contractor later supplied a relative's name and address. Gray filled out the death certificate with many "don't knows," and spelled the deceased's name as "U.G. Miller." Choteau undertaker Charles Connor shipped the body to Miller's brother in Dawson, Minnesota.

When the U.S. Bureau of Reclamation agreed to build Gibson Dam in the Sun River canyon starting in 1926, the water users in the Greenfield Irrigation District cheered, while a dude rancher in the canyon resisted.

"Government seeks to condemn Allan ranch, owners have refused $10,000 for resort property, complaint says," read the Dec. 2 Acantha headline.

"Condemnation proceedings against property owned by Ralph and Frances Allan in Sun River canyon have been filed in federal district court [in Great Falls] by Wellington D. Rankin, U.S. district attorney. The complaint asserts that the government has offered the Allans $10,000 for their property and the court is asked to approve transfer for this amount.

"The Allan ranch lies a short distance up the Sun River canyon from the point where Gibson Dam, a part of the Sun River Reclamation Project, is to be constructed. The land involved in the condemnation proceedings will be submerged when the dam is finally constructed and spring floodwaters are stored for use on the irrigation project later in the season.

"Although none of the land in the canyon has been surveyed, the Allan ranch consists of two tracts, one containing approximately 64 acres and the other about 95 acres. The ranch, in past seasons, has been one of the favorite camping places for parties spending the summer in the Sun River country and for hunters during the big game season," the Acantha reported.

"It is understood here that the Allans, who have operated a hotel and 'dude ranch' on their property in the canyon, have been holding out for $40,000 from the government. It is also reported that they have secured an option to purchase the tract embracing Sun River Hot Springs, about four miles above their present location. The springs, which attract hundreds of curious travelers and are popular with bathers, will not be submerged when the dam is completed.

"Other tracts in the area which will be submerged, it is reported, have already been purchased by the federal government without condemnation proceedings, and at the figures named by a board of appraisers of which T.O. Larson of Choteau was a member."

News of the negotiations was reported on May 19, 1927. "Appraisers fix value of Allan ranch at $18,500. The appraisement board appointed by Federal Judge Charles N. Pray to determine the value of the Ralph A. Allan ranch in the Sun River canyon has set the value of the ranch at $18,500. [About $267,720 in today's dollars.] Waters backed up by the Gibson Dam, now under construction, will cover the property, which has been used as a 'dude ranch,' to the depth of 100 feet or more, it is said.

"The government offered $10,000 for the property and the Allans asked $30,000. Unable to reach an agreement, the reclamation service started suit to condemn the property for public purposes. The board of appraisers which named the compromise figure was composed of Commissioner H.G. Pickett of Lewis and Clark County and George Hickman and A.M. Haty, both of Great Falls."

The news report on June 16 noted that Allan agreed to the compromise settlement. "Allan has already established a new camp farther up the canyon and directly across from Sun River Hot Springs. There he intends to erect a hotel, and will have cabins to rent. The river is to be bridged from the Allan camp across to the springs, one of the show spots of this section of the Rockies."

A front-page article on April 19, 1928, noted that Ralph Allan's "new and thoroughly modern" two-story hotel was nearly completed. Located seven miles upstream from the dam, it was on a plateau south of the hot springs and between the north and south forks of the river. The gates of the dam were closed in July 1929 and immediately the water rose to 50 feet above the original bed, submerging the old Allan site.

By Feb. 10, 1927, six months from the start of building Gibson Dam west of Augusta, more than 110 men were employed.

Dr. A.B. Gray of Choteau had the contract to provide medical services to Utah Construction Co. employees. He told the Acantha he would soon have a four-bed emergency hospital at the camp where his son Zahn would be in charge to render first aid.

Dr. H. Bateman treated a man at the dam site for a bad cut on his head in March, but the Acantha reported no other sickness until May when Clifford C. Combs, 24, succumbed to spinal meningitis with influenza as a contributory cause. His brother, who was also employed in the canyon, accompanied the body to Nebraska for burial.

The dam site became a tourist attraction. In April, for example, "Mr. and Mrs. L.E. Taylor, Mr. and Mrs. Phil I. Cole and Mrs. C.H. Porter were visitors at the Gibson Dam in Sun River canyon Monday. They report that the Utah Construction Co. is now employing about 175 men on the contract and that excellent progress is being made with the work. There is a crew at work digging a tunnel for the spillway. This tunnel is 30 feet in diameter and will be several hundred feet in length," the news stated.

The headline on a long article in June reported, "Crew of 300 at work." It noted that tunneling had stopped for the summer and the entire force was employed in top work. The construction camp was now a "regular town" complete with families of the employees. Narrow gauge tracks and gasoline dinkies, several steam shovels, and a couple of caterpillar tractors, were transporting supplies to the camp, and a big fleet of trucks was shortly going to start hauling cement for the concrete work that was expected to be poured over the summer.

A week later on June 23, 1927, the Acantha provided some technical notes on the massive project. The dam was a $1.8 million structure on the North Fork of the Sun River, 35 miles to the southwest of Choteau. It was designed as a "massive concrete arch type," with a crest length of about 900 feet and a maximum height of 195 feet. About 28 miles of transmission line from Montana Power Co. was built to Augusta.

"Excavation for the base and spillway were started as soon as the electric power was available early in December 1926. Contractors plan to complete all excavation for the dam and spillway by August 1927, and then pour concrete as long as the weather permits. The storage capacity is 90,000 acre-feet but provision has been made in the design so that drum gates may be installed on the spillway lip at some later date to increase the storage capacity to 105,000 acre-feet without raising the crest of the dam above the elevation provided for in the present contract. An area of 90,000 acres will be served by the Sun River Project when the dam is done," the Acantha reported.

There were no more reports until July when came mention of two babies born to UCC employees at Choteau hospital: a daughter, born prematurely to A. Dillard Parker and Thelma Parker on July 5, who died within hours; (the infant named Thelma was buried in the Augusta cemetery); and a son, Norman James, on June 30, born to George W. Pryor and Elsie Mae Pryor (surname spelled as "Prihar" on the birth certificate.)

In the fall of 1927 the news was of "winter work for woodchoppers." About 1,215 acres of land had to be cleared in the next 12 to 14 months. Invitations to bid on seven schedules were sent out where people could bid on any number. "The work must be started within 30 days after awards, and completed within 420 days," the report said. "All timber and brush is to be cut down and burned, leaving what will be the bed of the reservoir when the water is turned into it free of all brush and rubbish."

The second year of Gibson Dam's construction in 1928 was a quiet one news-wise, although with hundreds of men working in the Sun River Canyon, there was bound to be some casualties.

By June 1928, the Utah Construction Co. was running day and night shifts mixing concrete. About 50 percent of the dam was completed. During June, George P. Bowman, 69, a superintendent at the dam, died of bronchial pneumonia aggravated by gastric ulcers at Choteau hospital.

Because of a mild October, the workers made "exceptional progress" on the dam, the Acantha reported with, "nearly as much concrete being poured as at any time during the summer months." As a precaution, however, Assistant Supervisor A.D. Moir of the Lewis and Clark National Forest posted special fireguards where timber and brush were being cleared before being submerged behind the dam.

The Acantha reported the birth of a baby boy, George Jack O'Brien, to parents UCC employee John and Gladys O'Brien on Jan. 6, 1929, but a month later came the news of an accident at the dam.

"Young man killed in fall at Gibson Dam. Howard D. Lamb, aged 23, was almost instantly killed Tuesday morning at 9:30 at the Gibson Dam on Sun River. Death was due to a fall of about 90 feet in the shaft which, with the tunnel, is being constructed to take care of the overflow from the dam.

"What caused the young man to fall is not known as nothing broke or gave way. It is thought that he may have slipped from a scaffolding which is being used in lining the walls of the shaft and tunnel with cement. The total height of the shaft is about 190 feet and the unfortunate young man was about half way up when he fell.

"Dr. C.L. Dulaney of [Choteau] was immediately summoned and left in a short while after receipt of the message. He was accompanied by I.G. Lestrude as a hard trip over the snow-blocked roads was anticipated. The greatest difficulty was in reaching Augusta. From there no difficulty was experienced as snowplows were sent over the road in anticipation of the doctor's coming.

"Dr. Dulaney found that Lamb's skull was so badly fractured that portions of the brain were protruding. His legs, arms and back were also broken, and the doctor states that death must have been almost instantaneous.

"The body was taken to Great Falls yesterday and word of the accident was sent to relatives in Murray, Iowa, the young man's home.

"It was nearly 11 o'clock that night before Dulaney and Lestrude got back, and they had the assistance of Ranger C.V. Rubottom who came out with them. They experienced much more difficulty in coming down the canyon than in going up as the wind was blowing and the roads drifting rapidly. They came from Augusta by way of Simms."

By April the snow had melted in the Sun River Canyon and the engineers predicted that the dam would be completed by Aug. 1. That was proved correct, when in July the dam gates were closed and water had already risen to 50 feet above the original bed. Hikers had to use the new high trail between Mortimer and Big George gulches because the lower trail was now under water.

The Acantha picked up some news from the Fairfield Times in July that Al Udin "made quite a noteworthy purchase recently. He bought all the form material used in the construction work at Gibson Dam, a total of about 35,000 board-feet, and he will use it in building sheepsheds on his Spring Valley ranch. The material is in the form of panels and these are already coated with sheet metal and are thus ready to put together into a weather-proof building. Udin has already started to haul the material."

One more accidental death would forever be associated with building the dam in the final months of its three-year construction.

Superintendent Albert Paddock had overseen the building of Gibson Dam in the Sun River Canyon for nearly three years.

The concrete structure required hundreds of workers and so in April 1929 Paddock, 45, was looking forward to its finish in July.

Fate intervened. The River Press reported on the fatal accident, but it included several errors that the Acantha later corrected.

"Foreman of dam killed. Great Falls — Struck by the body of a workman who lost his balance 60 feet above, Albert Paddock, superintendent of construction on the Sun River government dam near here, was killed there recently.

"[Harold Weismann] had been working on a guy wire, about half way up the 240-foot steel tower on the dam. Paddock was about 60 feet below him, sitting on the 'bail' of the 'skip' or lift. [Weismann] lost his balance and fell as he stepped into the tower. The superintendent's body broke his 100-foot drop but Paddock's ribs were broken and he was injured internally by the force of the impact and the resulting 40-foot fall. He lived about an hour."

The accident happened on April 20. The Acantha's report in the April 25 edition read: "Harold Weismann tells of accident at Gibson Dam. Did not fall to ground with Superintendent Paddock, who was killed, clothes catch in tower. In the accident which happened at the Gibson Dam on Sun River last Saturday morning, in which Superintendent A.E. Paddock was so severely injured that he died an hour later, Harold Weismann, who miraculously escaped with his life after falling over 100 feet, did not fall to the ground and strike on the superintendent's body, thus saving his own, as was first reported.

"Weismann, who is 20 years of age, [he was listed as 18 on the 1930 census] and a son of Mr. and Mrs. P.C. Thor Weismann of Great Falls, lies in the Choteau hospital, and by Monday had so far recovered from his injuries and regained his faculties that he was able to tell clearly just how the accident happened and how his own life was saved in the outstanding fall down the 240-foot steel tower.

"'We had just gone to work and I was in the crow's nest of the tower where my work is to give signals for material to be brought up the tower on the skip. I looked down the tower and saw that the drops on the end of the counterbalances of the boom were caught in one of the tower guy lines about 60 feet below me. As the men who work in the tower frequently do, I took hold of the cable which hoists the skip and wrapped my legs about it and started to slide down the cable. I had not gone far when I noticed the cable was wet from the rain the night before and realized that it would probably be dangerous for me to try to go the remainder of the distance down. I therefore stopped myself and reached out with one hand for the frame of the tower. Just as I did this, the cable started up suddenly and I lost my hold and fell.'

"The young man explains that he was conscious that he was falling and knew he hit something but did not know just what it was. What he did hit was Paddock, who evidently had observed the same trouble which Weismann had, and stepped into the skip and started up. He had risen about 40 feet from the ground when Weismann, falling like a plummet, crashed into him. The skip turned over and let Paddock through and he fell to the concrete below. In striking the superintendent and the skip the youth was diverted from his downward course and just a little way below the skip his heavy clothing caught in the framework of the tower and held him there until fellow workmen rescued him.

"The young man is grieved over the death of the superintendent. He states that Paddock was held in the highest esteem by the workmen and that he had a remarkable faculty of being able to get along with the men and accomplish results."

Published in the Choteau Acantha June 19, 26, July 3, 10, 17, 24, 31, Aug. 7, 2019.

19

Recalling the Elk Creek Cabin Fire

1927

Lewis and Clark National Forest officials had already assigned a ranger and completed some type of housing in the Elk Creek Ranger District by 1908, a few years after the forest's creation.

Located 15 miles south and west of Augusta on the South Fork of the Sun River, the Elk Creek station became the home of a handful of rangers.

Forest officials completed a new ranger's building on Elk Creek, as part of a $60,000 forest-wide construction project in 1923. Ranger Sam F. Harris from Missoula was in charge when the station became more than a simple mention in the news.

"The ranger station at Elk Creek and all its contents were destroyed by fire of unknown origin Tuesday afternoon at about five o'clock. There was no forest fire near the station and there had been no fire in the station stove since noon.

"The station had been occupied by Ranger Harris and his wife, recently appointed to this forest from Missoula. Ranger Harris was away on duty at the time and Mrs. Harris discovered the fire when she saw smoke as she was on the way home from a nearby ranch where she had gone for milk. The building was in ruins when she reached it," the Acantha reported.

Harris was made of tough stuff, if this article was any

indication. On Feb. 17, 1927, it began, "Life of forest ranger not always a joy in winter. Sam Harris of Elk Creek station shivered through this season in a tent.

"The life of one of Uncle Sam's forest rangers is frequently tough during the summer season, particularly when the timber's dry and the fires are many, but it is anything but a joy, or would be to the average mortal, in winter, snowed-in miles from nowhere even in a good tight cabin. And when Lady Luck frowns, burns your cabin in the fall and leaves you to spend the most severe winter in years in a tent with only your thoughts for company, you could be pardoned perhaps for growling a bit at your fate.

"That's what happened to Ranger Sam Harris of the Elk Creek station, Lewis and Clark forest, this year, and the kind of a man Mr. Harris is, is best illustrated by his comment upon the prank Dame Fortune played on him. In his own words, Ranger Harris 'got a kick out of it,' even though he often pounded out his reports on his typewriter, sitting bundled up in his mackinaw, his feet plunged for protection from drafts into an empty cracker carton.

"Ranger Harris likes eggs and butter, in fact can do very well without other eatables so long as he has them, but when he left them off the stove they'd freeze and when he put them atop the stove for safety's sake, the eggs would cook and the butter melt, while water froze in a bucket a few feet away.

"But Ranger Harris stuck it out until last week when he was called to Choteau for a month's office detail. And this summer he'll have a new home in the hills, started last fall, but abandoned for the winter when early frost caught the workers. And Mr. Harris is hoping for an early spring.

"Mr. Harris's station burned last fall one day while he and Mrs. Harris were away, and they returned to find their home a heap of ashes. A new station was started then, but the work of getting in material and erecting the building was slow, and frost put a stop to operations before the concrete work could be completed. Mr. Harris is doing most of the work himself, to keep within the appropriation allowed by the government, and is hoping that spring will break soon for if it does, he can get some help from other rangers before another season requires their constant presence on their own districts."

The Acantha reported in July 1927 that Harris, his wife, Grace, and their son, Sam Jr., 3, were still living in the tent. The new ranger station was only about 70 percent complete in February 1928, but the family moved into the cabin eventually.

Mrs. Harris gave birth to their second son while the family lived at the Elk Creek station. The Lewis and Clark and Jefferson forests consolidated a year later in 1931, and in 1933, Sam Harris was transferred to the Blackfoot District of the Helena National Forest. The forest archaeologist Mark Bodily said the only building that is left of the original Elk Creek Ranger Station is the tack shed, which is still administratively being used. The original residential/administrative cabin is gone, along with a host of memories. 🏔

Published in the Choteau Acantha January 10, 2018.

20

Dr. Oscar Kenck Speaks of Mountain Lore

1933

The audience listened intently to what the highly-respected Augusta dentist said in March 1933, a speech that reflected his love of the Sun River country west of where he made his home.

"A call for the conservation of wildlife and the protection of mountain areas from the intrusion of civilization was sounded last night at the regular meeting of the Choteau Lions Club by Dr. Oscar A. Kenck, Augusta dentist and former practitioner in Choteau. The subject of Dr. Kenck's address was 'Our Mountains,'" the Acantha reported.

"He went back first to the early days and told of the slaughter of elk, like buffalo for their hides. Later, he said, came the tie cutters for railroad construction and the woodcutters. The gradual inroad of civilization into the mountains was traced. In that connection he mentioned the geological survey, the construction of reservoirs and diversion dams, the building of roads, the coming of guides and finally the erection of cabins and summer homes.

"He mentioned the Sun River area in particular and expressed disapproval of the Forest Service's construction of the new road to Benchmark on the South Fork of Sun River. The region, he said, had been a wilderness and a game paradise. This coming fall, he predicted, will witness the coming of a thousand cars into that area and a consequent depletion of its game resources. In this connection, he showed the efforts which have been put forth to propagate wildlife by the sportsmen and lovers of nature, saying that it was but a comparatively few years ago that the first fish were planted above the Sun River Diversion Dam.

"He favored the creation of a primitive area in this region as is provided by federal law, and said that both Choteau and Augusta have a great natural resource in this region and that the people are commencing to wake up to this fact and should realize it still more fully.

"Before long, Forest Service officials will be here to consider the matter of the creation of this primitive area, he stated, and he urged that the people familiarize themselves with the need for wildlife conservation and the dangers that confront it and be prepared to support the primitive area plan."

Kenck, himself, had made an inroad into the wilderness. He built a cabin in 1924 about a half-mile west of the first road into the Benchmark country. At his ranch on the Dearborn River, he created a fish farm, one that could have stocked trout above the Diversion Dam, before the enterprise suffered when the muskrats moved in. It's where his son, Richard, learned to trap.

In November 1907 the Acantha reported, "Chas. Cowell, who returned Monday from a hunting trip, reports that he met Dr. O.A. Kenck's party away back in the wilds, and that the doctor was down on his luck, not having killed an elk. He said that he was going to have one, if he had to winter in the hills. The 'doc' may turn out [to be] a veritable old Man of the Mountains."

In June 1950, the Montana State Dental Association selected him as the "outstanding dentist of the half century" in terms of length of practice and high quality of service to his people, the Acantha reported.

The Great Falls Tribune wrote about him in 1962, noting that he had only retired four years ago, having come to Augusta in 1905. His legacy, he died in 1965, has come down to the present in several ways. In 1969 his dental equipment was donated to the Montana Historical Society for a Main Street exhibit, titled, "Territory Junction." In 1972 his old dental office in Augusta became an information and referral service station for Augusta residents and an outpost office for the various agency and service representatives who visited Augusta.

And in June 2009, his old cabin at the end of the Benchmark Road was dedicated, having been donated in 2004 and remodeled into a recreational rental cabin operated by the U.S. Forest Service. His biography, "Montana Treasure," was published in 2004. And his old "traveling" dental parlor built on wheels, is housed at the Augusta Area Museum.

Published in the Choteau Acantha December 23, 2020.

— 21 —

Rabbit Drive

Fred Willson arrived in Choteau from North Dakota in June 1934, knowing that he had big shoes to fill as the new Teton County Extension agent.

He replaced Robert Clarkson who had enjoyed a 16-year stint in the office and who moved to Helena to head the Rural Rehabilitation Program. Clarkson's office assistants, Iona Davidson and Mable Caskey, helped Willson, who hit the ground running. He said, "The most immediate pressing problem seen to be ahead is the prosecution of the hopper poisoning campaign."

The tale on the grasshopper eradication campaign is for another time. Instead, a report on Willson's other target, jackrabbits, follows.

Willson on Dec. 19, 1935, reported in the Acantha, "Jackrabbit Menace is Looming; Control Methods Suggested."

"During the last two years jackrabbits have increased at an alarming rate," he wrote. "Unless something is done this winter to control these pests, thousands of dollars in damage to crops will be the consequences next summer. Rabbits have the habit of appearing in cycles of abundance. Occasionally they are beset by disease, which destroys most of them.

"How much damage does a rabbit do? Tests in Arizona have shown that 12 jackrabbits will eat as much as a full-grown ewe, that 59 jackrabbits will eat enough to keep a cow a year. There are two things that we can do to destroy these pests. 'Drives' during the winter months is one of the best ways of controlling jackrabbits, however, it takes approximately 100 well-organized people to conduct a successful drive.

"I believe that in the communities where rabbits are most numerous it would be possible to put on a few drives during the winter months. If I can be of any assistance in helping organizing jackrabbit drives, feel free to call upon me. "Poisoning is also effective. The bait is placed along the trails used by rabbits. Care must be taken so as not to poison livestock," Willson wrote, and then gave a recipe for soaking strychnine sulphate in alfalfa hay as bait.

The next week, the Acantha described a third remedy, how the county's 4-H clubs had waged war on rabbits by holding a rodent control contest. In the contest between May 1, 1935, and Nov. 1, 1935, 66 boys and girls from 11 clubs killed 1,964 rabbits.

Awards to the clubs and individuals were determined on the basis of points for the animals turned in. The points were: ground hogs, 50; jackrabbits, 50; prairie dogs, 30; gophers, 20; moles, 20; crows, 50; magpies, 50; and crow or magpie eggs, 10 points each.

The full tails of gophers, ground hogs and prairie dogs, two ears of jackrabbits, two front feet of moles, heads of magpies and crows, and crow or magpie eggs were required to be submitted to the local leaders.

Eighteen kids qualified for prizes. The children turned in evidence of 7,105 gophers, 1,964 rabbits, 33 ground hogs, five moles, 357 magpies, 262 magpie eggs, 145 crows and 80 crow eggs during that seven-month period. Alvin Reiquam, the head of the 4-H Council's rodent control committee, conservatively estimated a saving of $10,000 in crops.

Clyde Schultz, the son of Martin Schultz of the Diamond

Valley community, garnered the highest points for boys and next in line was Betty Brownell Erickson, daughter of Max Brownell of the Pendroy community.

The boy winners included Schultz, Ole Vervick, Arthur Konen, Howard Riphenburg, Otto Bremer, Jimmie Anderson, Donald Newman, Glen Laubach, Arthur Habel, Billy Reiquam, Eldon Reiquam and Herbert Hanson.

The girl winners were Erickson, Christie Swanson, Julia Rowland, Lois Swenson, Cora Otness and Hope Johnson. They all had at least 5,000 points.

The club rank was Dandy Decorators of Pendroy, first; Diamond Valley 4-H Livestock, second; Greenfield Certified Seed Potato, third; Fairview Baby Chick, fourth. Other clubs were Greenfield Home Improvement, Scissor Snippers, Collins Boosters, 4-H Future Farmers, Bole Corn and Poultry Club, Willing Workers and Seven Cooks. The children split $50, with the grand prize being $5 for individuals; the others a lesser amount, and $10 for the high club. More than 70 businesses donated prizes as well.

While the 4-H Council planned another rodent contest, Willson worked to schedule his preferred remedy, a rabbit drive, set for February 1936, which turned out to be the coldest February ever recorded in Choteau.

At a fall meeting it was decided that the contest for 1936 would have its beginning on Nov. 1, 1935. The Acantha stated, "One of the main reasons for this is that the club members will have a chance during the winter months to make raids on jackrabbits which are regarded as increasing to damaging proportions." Willson pointed out that killing rabbits in winter was very desirable as it prevented increases in the spring and summer months.

White-tailed jackrabbits are not rabbits. They are hares that can weigh more than six pounds. They turn white in the winter except for the edges of their unusually long ears.

The first rabbit-news report came on Jan. 30, 1936, from the Beck community southeast of Choteau. "Beck Community Ends Rabbit Drive With Dance and Program. A drive to reduce the large number of jackrabbits in the Beck community and sponsored by the Beck Home Demonstration Club, came to a close last Thursday evening, having been in progress since Dec. 24. The climax of this campaign was the awarding of prizes to the winners of first, second and third places, followed by a program and dance in the Beck schoolhouse.

"Clarence Lehnerz took first honors with 93 pairs of ears, William Wietke was second with 84 pairs and Willard Asmus was third with 34.

"The program rendered was as follows: harmonica band by Plainview School, cornet solo by George Gamradt, accordion solo by Asmus and group singing of 'The Music Goes Round and Round,' as the closing number. Dancing was enjoyed until a late hour and a chop suey supper served at midnight."

The next time rabbits were in the news was on Feb. 13 when the Pinnell Fur Co. in Choteau placed a "furs wanted" ad in the Acantha. "Wanted 5,000 jackrabbits. Special notice, owing to weather conditions and other factors, we have raised the price to six cents instead of five cents as offered last week. Remember, we must have rabbits by Feb. 25 to supply contract."

A Feb. 20 news item noted that jackrabbit hunting could prove to be a profitable business. "Great truckloads of jackrabbits are being taken to Harlem by farmers finding it a profitable winter business to kill the rabbits, which are bringing from five cents unskinned to 10 cents for dry hides on the Harlem market. Besides adding materially to the farmers' income, the prairies are being rid of one of the region's worst pests."

In the same Acantha edition Willson announced a rabbit drive, although temperatures each night had begun to be well below zero. The temperature plunged to 50 below zero on Feb. 15.

"Plans are now being worked out by County Agent Fred Willson for a rabbit drive southeast of Choteau next Sunday. The cooperation of citizens generally, sportsmen, farmers, Boy Scouts and others interested is invited by Mr. Willson for this undertaking which is felt will not only do much good for agriculture but will also afford an hour or two of healthful recreation and net someone a little cash as there is a demand at this time for rabbit pelts and carcasses.

"The plan is to have drivers assemble at the courthouse from where departure will occur at 9 o'clock. At least 50 or 60 individuals should be on hand to make the drive a success, the agent explained, and they should leave dogs and guns at home and carry a club or possibly a noisemaking device. On the grounds, a walk of not over two or two and a half miles is contemplated, as coverage of a large territory is not contemplated.

"The aim will be to complete the drive in the forenoon so that it will not interfere with the basketball game scheduled for 3 p.m. at the county high gym. County snow fence will be strung out to make a corral."

With 7.5 inches of snow on the ground as the rabbit drive neared, Choteau folk contended with unrelenting below-zero nighttime temperatures. On Saturday, Feb. 22, it snowed another 2.5 inches.

Willson decided to postpone the rabbit drive set for Feb. 23, 1936, when too few men and boys showed up during the record cold weather.

On Feb. 27, the Acantha announced, "The rabbit drive southeast of Choteau, which was to be last Sunday morning, has been postponed until this coming Sunday and will occur in the afternoon.

"Not enough men turned out last Sunday to make the event a success, so it was decided to try again. About 25 showed up by 9 o'clock last Sunday but it was felt that 75 or 100 would be necessary. Some came after 10 o'clock but it was too late then because it was desired to have the drive over with, so that it would not interfere with the plans of those who wanted to attend the basketball game in the afternoon.

"It is thought that more will be able to turn out for the afternoon. Departure will be from the courthouse at 2 p.m. County snow fence has been put up to form a corral. Dogs and guns must be left at home. Participants will not have to walk over one and a half to two miles, according to plans."

Willson targeted rabbits, he said, when it appeared they had "increased at an alarming rate," during the previous two years. He decided that winter killing was desirable because it prevented increases in the spring and fall. White-tailed jackrabbits are capable of having as many as four litters each year.

February 1936 holds the record for the coldest ever February in Choteau, with an average temperature of -5.8 degrees. Willson's decision to delay the drive was fortuitous. A Chinook rolled in on Feb. 27 and by March 1, the temperature rose to 52 and all the snow melted.

The Acantha reported on the rabbit drive on March 5 in an article, "Wise Rabbits Duck; Clubs Thump Others."

"Not many rabbits but heaps of fun was the net result of the drive Sunday afternoon. About 55 boys and 20 adults were out and the country covered lay east of the highway just south of the Teton River bridge from Choteau on the Freeman & Elliott and Pete Sandmo ranches.

"The rabbits were herded into a corral improvised from snow fence, and it was estimated that about 50 were run into the wings of the enclosure. The boys rushed the rabbits before the wings could be drawn together and this resulted in the escape of half the number. There were scads of rabbits, said Willson, who directed the enterprise, but not enough herders; consequently many rabbits 'ducked.'

"'This was somewhat of an experiment,' Willson related, and it showed that there should have been at least 150 out, with more adults. Firearms and dogs were tabooed."

The rodent control contest results on Nov. 5, 1936, were: rabbits, 1,964 in 1935 and 2,863 in 1936; and gophers, 7,105 in 1935 and 9,377 in 1936. The 4-H club members also brought in magpies, crows, crow eggs, ground hogs, magpie eggs and moles. However, because of the danger of bubonic plague, no points were given in 1936 for ground squirrels, jackrabbits or prairie dogs.

The three highest points obtained by girls and boys in the county were: Julia Rowland, Pendroy Pals, 31,550; Christie Swanson, Pendroy Pals, 6,500; Alma Camden, Scissor Snippers, 6,100; Joe Tackes, Greenfield Certified Seed, 51,520; Frank Campbell, Harmony, 43,760; and Leland Rowley, Muddy Creek, 25,710.

By Dec. 3, Willson was back to recommending putting out grain or alfalfa bundles dipped in poison to control rabbits. He continued as the Extension agent until he took a job in 1939 as the manager of the Northern Montana Ag Experimental Station.

Rabbit drives were mentioned in the Acantha two more times. On Jan. 11, 1945, Pendroy News reporter Mrs. Carl Gulbrandsen reported, "Four Valierians dropped in Sunday at Jay Gitchel's and staged a rabbit drive. They bagged 40 of them, which was excellent considering the scarcity of rabbits these days, but then, Gitchels have an ideal grove for rabbit conventions."

On Sept. 15, 1993, the Acantha published Lois

Crabtree's photo of a "Teton County Intercommunity Rabbit Drive" undertaken in February 1925 in which the Beck community won with 1,914 rabbit ears.

Published in the Choteau Acantha March 13, 20, 27, 2019.

Bear Kills Joseph Chincisian

Sheepherder Joseph Chincisian has the distinction of being the only person reported killed by a grizzly bear along the Rocky Mountain Front, but his death in 1947 was barely mentioned in the local news at the time.

It took the late Ben East, a prolific writer of the outdoors, in 1967, and Larry Kaniut, an author of bear tales who found East's article in 2001, to resurrect the tragic events from the local residents in the first case, and from the Outdoor Life Magazine archives in the second.

Chincisian had emigrated from Austria or Romania in 1912 and in the 1920 federal census he was a hired hand on the Clint Peer ranch near Cascade. He shows up again in the 1940 census where he is a hired hand with 13 other hired men working for the Mosher ranch 16 miles south of Augusta. Stephen Mosher Sr. had died and his widow, Amelia, was the head of the household with her sons, Stephen Jr., 26, and Richard, 24, working as the ranch managers. Chincisian's birth year could have been 1882, 1884, 1886 or 1890, based on the records.

The Acantha had two short articles. The Oct. 2, 1947, edition reported, "At Augusta this week, Joseph [or Josif or Josef] Chincisian, 63, a sheepherder, was critically injured when a bear clawed his face, neck and arms and almost removed his scalp. The man was rushed from the Mosher ranch to a Great Falls hospital."

The second article on Oct. 23, reported, "Augusta

rancher kills big grizzly. Dick Bean, 72-year-old Augusta rancher, last week killed a huge grizzly near Augusta on Fall Creek believed to have been the same bear, which killed a sheepherder two weeks ago.

"Bean was searching for strayed cattle when the bear charged him. The rancher fired once, hitting the grizzly over the eye. The bear was one of the largest ever seen in the area, observers said."

That was it, until writer East picked up the story. Kaniut republished the story in "Bear Tales for the Ages, From Alaska and Beyond."

The first chapter, "A Bad One," starts with a comment that the "phenomenal tale is about a cunning grizzly, a shepherd's protective attitude and his determination to save his sheep."

The nine pages that follow are indeed a harrowing tale, and how East got all the information died with him, although his personal papers, archived at the University of Michigan in Ann Arbor, may contain the information. (The Great Falls newspaper might have an article but that was not checked.)

Joe was minding 2,000 sheep near Cuniff Creek and was aware that a sheep-killing bear was around. He had accidentally shot his dog, when stalking a sheep-eating bear some time earlier in the fall. One of his campsites was a vacant, tumbledown homesteader's one-room cabin, but he also had a sheepherder's wagon up the hill.

He heard a disturbance, and with no fear of bears, he followed the sheep trail to the herd, where a grizzly was feeding on a dead sheep on a gravel bar at the creek.

The grizzly charged and Joe got off a shot with a .30/40 Krag rifle that missed, and then the bear was on him. Joe's blood spattered on the gravel and the medical report would later show that his skull was broken, he was scalped, and he had puncture wounds in his upper right arm.

While he was unconscious, the bear dragged him to a spot where it covered the man with leaves and earth. Joe came to and crawled all the way to the shack about 100 feet away, but he then found the strength to walk to his wagon, leaving bloody marks along the way.

He lay in his bed there until about noon, then started walking to the Henry Heydweiller place a mile and a half away on the North Fork of the Dearborn River.

He stayed on his feet and climbed over two fences on his way but collapsed a half-mile from the ranch. That Saturday morning, Sept. 27, Heydweiller had ridden into the hills looking for the sheep-killing bear and he saw the wounded man lying in the grass as he rode toward his place.

Joe was still alive, but his torn scalp and ear hung in a dried, bloody flap over his face and his brain was exposed where a piece of skull the size of a silver dollar was missing. Heydweiller raced to his ranch, dismounted and dove into his pickup and set off to get Joe.

The half-conscious Chincisian, with Heydweiller's assistance, managed to get into the bed of the rancher's pickup before he raced to the Mosher ranch, located 16 miles south of Augusta, where the other ranch hands were gathered for supper. The grizzly bear had ripped Chincisian's scalp and the hours-long delay in being rescued had left his scalp too hardened to be put back in place.

With Chincisian's head bandaged and his body steadied by a fellow ranch hand in the back seat, Richard "Dick" Mosher drove his car to Deaconess Hospital in Great Falls, 65 miles away.

East wrote that Mosher led a party up to Chincisian's camp the next morning. They reconstructed what happened by tracking the man's blood, noting that the bear had killed two sheep. They also found a bit of the man's skull.

Bruce Neal, a state game warden and former government tracker, investigated the attack. Chincisian's rifle had its bolt open and an ejected shell lay nearby, but the bullet had missed its target.

Before Mosher headed to Great Falls, he told the hired hands to move the sheep down to a corral and open shed a mile nearer the Mosher ranch buildings. Sheepherder Theodore Olsen from Augusta took charge of the herd, but was told to not venture out during the night if something happened. Around midnight a bear killed a ewe, dragged it over a four-foot-high fence and buried it near a tree, then laid down against the shed for hours before leaving without feeding on the ewe.

East said Neal was convinced that the bear used the sheep as bait and was waiting for Olsen to venture out to ambush him.

Chincisian lived for 10 days, but despite brain surgery, and the best of care, he died on Oct. 7, 1947. He had fainted before arriving at the hospital and never regained consciousness. He is buried in Augusta Cemetery under a granite marker, "Josif Chincisian, 1882-1947." Choteau resident Al Wiseman said in 2018 that he and his father dug the man's grave. Wiseman was 11 and the family lived in Gilman near Augusta at the time. He said his dad got $20 for the work, but it took three days because the ground was "cement gravel."

The local ranchers in Augusta and along the Dearborn hunted for the bear throughout the fall. Trappers' dogs lost the scent on bare ground, and in spite of killing some black bears, the hunters did not get a grizzly and gave up.

The Acantha reported that neighboring rancher Dick Bean shot a grizzly a couple of weeks after the mauling, and that it was probably the right bear.

But East said the dead one had two missing, but healed,

middle toes in a front foot, and the tracks along Cuniff Creek showed no signs of that.

The bear never came back to feed on its three sheep kills nor did it bother the herd again. However, Mosher was "convinced that, unless some hunter miles from the attack scene back in the mountains shot him later and was unaware of what he had bagged, the grizzly that struck down Chincisian that dark September night was never killed."

The Oct. 2, 1947, Acantha had a front-page story about "wild bears being found in almost every kind of habitat and environment locally this year," because an early frost had killed berries, their usual food source.

Besides mentioning Chincisian as being critically injured, the newspaper reported that Evan Thompson killed a small, 85-pound brown bear, wandering on the Bob Miller property on the north side of Choteau. He needed four shots to do it, the news said, adding, "Robert Van Scherpenzeel, Choteau, recently ran over a bear on the Choteau-Augusta highway. Because the bear was only slightly hit, Van Scherpenzeel turned the car around and ran over the big bear another time, since he carried no gun. The bear finally walked away, still only slightly injured."

Published in the Choteau Acantha February 7, 14, 2018.

Two Die in Korean Conflict

Sometimes a story does not have a satisfactory ending, and one might conclude that from the tale of two young men from Fairfield killed in the 1950s Korean Conflict.

Gene Henry Lease, 18, and Oliver Martin Fields, 24, died on Sept. 26, 1950, and Nov. 27, 1950, respectively, in two different battles. They were the only two servicemen from Teton County who died in that three-year-long unofficial war, although many local men served. Dean Sala from Choteau, who worked at Breen Oil Co., nearly died, and spent months undergoing treatment for machine gun wounds in his arms and legs. Sala was in a Marine unit of 45 men and all but three of them died, the Acantha reported. Montana had 137 casualties in total.

Lease's parents had come to Fairfield in 1928. Born in Great Falls on Oct. 27, 1931, Lease attended Fairfield schools and would have been a high school senior in the fall of 1950.

He was an outstanding FFA chapter member winning many awards, and had won four prizes for his sheep exhibits that summer at the North Montana State Fair. He won first place on Fairfield's FFA basketball team the previous two years in the district tourney. He was a member of the Greenfield Roundup Saddle Club, and the past two summers had taken an active part in amateur rodeo, riding bareback bucking broncs.

Lease was a popular and accomplished Fairfield High

School student. He and his classmate Douglas Crary joined the Marine Reserves in Shelby and spent two weeks of training at Oceanside, California, in June 1950, the newspaper noted.

On July 13, 1950, the news included a report on Montana's first high school rodeo, set in Augusta for July 16. More than 51 boys and 13 girls entered, according to the rodeo committee. Fairfield's entries were Crary, Lease, Audrey Crabtree and Boyd Jensen. Augusta planned to sponsor a high school rodeo every year as a non-profit venture for the entire state. Lease placed fourth in bareback riding.

In August the Shelby Marine Reserve group received orders to report for further training on Aug. 9. The group included Lease, Crary, Levi Boss, Sherrill Vance and Bob Huntsinger under Commanding Officer Capt. Arthur Zimmerman. They traveled to Camp Pendleton, California.

The Oct. 12 Acantha announced the tragic news that Pfc. Lease, only son of Mr. and Mrs. Henry Lease, was killed in action in Korea on Sept. 26. The entire Fairfield community was deeply shocked, the news noted, and it wanted answers.

Lease left for overseas duty on Sept. 1 and landed at Kobe, Japan, after spending 20 days aboard ship. He was with the first Marine division that made the Inchon landing and recaptured Seoul.

On Oct. 19, the Acantha reported that Lease's death brought protests regarding training in service. "Better training for Marine Reserves is demanded in a petition presented to Rep. Wesley A. D'Ewart by Fairfield residents who asked that he transmit their request to the Secretary of Defense," the news reported.

Their petition stated that Lease was sent into combat and killed after only 54 hours of training and they expressed the hope that "careful study of this case may prevent further incidents of this nature." D'Ewart said he expected a similar petition from Shelby residents. Several Toole County members of the Marine Reserve unit were also killed in action, (of six men killed in the three-year period) within two months of their departure from home.

Their outrage stemmed from a Sept. 20 news report saying that the Camp Pendleton commander had stated, "Only combat veterans would be sent to Korea as replacements while other Marine reservists would receive at least a four-week training course."

The petition explained that Lease attended two 10-day summer training periods and attended twice monthly reserve meetings before he was called with his unit to active duty on Aug. 8. He arrived at Camp Pendleton on Aug. 12, sailed from the United States on Aug. 27, arrived at Kobe on Sept. 14, left for Korea on Sept. 17 and was killed in action nine days later, having received 54 hours of training.

The Acantha reported that Lease had had some combat training in Japan on Sept. 14-17, when the actual combat session was held with eight hours of training and eight hours off, and Lease received 10 hours of sleep during the period, a petition of protest stated. Moreover, the 10-day summer training course at Camp Pendleton, California, he had attended, "included the time the Marine unit left Shelby until they were home, which took three days at least. That left seven actual days of training."

"The Department of Defense certainly owes these people an explanation and must take steps at once to improve the training program," said Rep. D'Ewart.

The Acantha reported that Brigadier General Merrill B. Twining, Camp Pendleton commander, said that all reservists called to active duty were not handled in the same way. ... "Only a veteran combat man who is in top condition is placed in a replacement draft at once." The petitioners declared that Lease did not receive that consideration.

"Don't send our boys to die without a chance," said the petitioners, who the Acantha did not name. "Your signature may protect some other mother's son."

No more information about Lease appeared in the Acantha until July 12, 1951, when it reported that Gene's father, Henry, who operated the local lumber yard, had donated the "Gene Lease Memorial [traveling] Trophy" to the second annual Montana Championship High School Rodeo, to be given to the school that had the highest number of points for its entrants. The named trophy was used through at least 1955.

On June 5, 1952, the Acantha reported, "A large crowd attended the annual Memorial Day services held in the [Fairfield High School] gym Friday morning." The American Legion and the Veterans of Foreign Wars and their auxiliaries sponsored this service each year.

"During the service a Silver Star award was presented posthumously to the parents of Pfc. Gene Lease who was killed in action Sept. 26, 1950, in Korea. Major Arthur Zimmerman, USMCR, presented the medal to Mrs. Henry Lease following the reading of the citation by Capt. Ron Rice, USMCR. Lease was killed during the battle of Seoul when with complete disregard for his own safety, he went through intense enemy fire to rescue his commanding officer who had been critically wounded. Through his actions the life of his commanding officer was saved but Lease was mortally wounded."

The Defense POW/MIA Accounting Agency website notes: "On Sept. 26, 1950, the U.S. 7th Marine Regiment was fighting North Korean troops in the vicinity of Seoul. Battles took place in villages near Seoul, but the hard-fought areas of true strategic importance were the hills surrounding the city, particularly Hill 296 and Hill 338, which overlooked the roads approaching Seoul. Ultimately, United Nations troops gained control of these areas and pushed the North Koreans out of the capital city.

"Pfc. Gene Harry (sic) Lease, who joined the U.S. Marine Corps from Montana, served with Company D, 2nd Battalion, 7th Marine Regiment, 1st Marine Division. He was killed in action on Sept. 26, 1950, during the UN's effort to push North Korean forces out of Seoul. Lease's body could not be recovered at the time of his loss, and later searches for his remains were unsuccessful. He has not been associated with any remains recovered from the area after the war. He is still unaccounted-for. Today, Lease is memorialized on the Courts of the Missing at the National Memorial Cemetery of the Pacific, in Honolulu, Hawaii.

"Based on all information available, DPAA assessed the individual's case to be in the analytical category of 'Under Review.'" A family member submitted DNA to the Korean War Project in the hopes that someday a match could be made.

Lease's cousin, Richard, organized a graveside ceremony with veterans in 2011 in Sunset Memorial Cemetery outside Fairfield. Lease's gravemarker lies near his father's marker, (he died in 1952), but only a memorial capsule is buried there.

Oliver Martin Fields, 24, died on Nov. 27, 1950, in the battle of the Chongchon River.

The Dec. 28, 1950, Acantha reported that Sergeant First Class Fields was killed in action in Korea. He was the brother of Mrs. Mabel (Raymond) Hagen and Oscar Fields (his twin brother) both of Fairfield. His other siblings lived elsewhere. His stepfather, August Schwartz, and his half-brother, Allen Schwartz, also lived in Fairfield. The death notice said Fields had a wife in Portland, but that information could not be verified.

Fields was a native of Rudyard, where his father had died and his mother had remarried. The family moved to Fairfield in 1940 and Oliver attended Fairfield High School. His mother died in 1947 and was buried in St. Paul Cemetery and in that year Oliver enlisted in the Army.

The Acantha noted he had served four years in the U.S. Navy during World War II, but that could not be confirmed. After enlisting in the army he was stationed at Fort Lewis, Washington, before going to Korea. He had been overseas with an engineering unit since July 17, 1950.

On Feb. 15, 1951, the Acantha reported that Fields, who had previously been listed as missing in action, now was reported killed in Korea. No other articles were written about the young soldier, although his sister, Mabel [Hagen], filed a probate case on Aug. 20, 1955. Fields had $288.34 in a cash account, and after court expenses, a balance of $147.70 was disbursed to his brothers and sisters. By 1955, all of his siblings had moved away from Fairfield.

The Defense POW/MIA Accounting Agency website states: "By mid-November 1950, U.S. and allied forces had advanced to within approximately 60 miles of the Yalu River, the border between North Korea and China. On Nov. 25, 300,000 Chinese Communist Forces (CCF) 'volunteers' suddenly and fiercely counterattacked after crossing the Yalu. The 2nd Infantry Division, located the farthest north of any units at the Chongchon River, could not halt the CCF advance and was ordered to withdraw to defensive positions at Sunchon. As the division pulled back from Kunu-ri toward Sunchon, its men conducted an intense rearguard action while also fighting to break through well-defended roadblocks set up by CCF infiltrators. The withdrawal was not complete until Dec. 1, and the 2nd Infantry Division suffered extremely heavy casualties in the process.

"Sfc. Fields, who joined the U.S. Army from Montana,

served with Co. C, 2nd Engineer Combat Battalion, 2nd Infantry Division. He was killed in action on Nov. 27, 1950, as his unit supported defensive positions of the 9th Infantry Regiment on the west bank of the Chongchon River against a ferocious CCF attack. Records indicate that Army Graves Registration Services buried Sfc. Fields in plot 3-10-536 of the United Nations Military Command Cemetery near Pyongyang; however, his remains have not been identified among those returned to U.S. custody. Sfc. Fields is memorialized on the Courts of the Missing at the National Memorial Cemetery of the Pacific in Honolulu, Hawaii.

"Based on all information available, DPAA assessed the individual's case to be in the analytical category of 'Under Review.'" For his leadership and valor, Fields was posthumously awarded the Bronze Star, among other medals.

As of 2009, his twin brother was living in Washington. A family member submitted a DNA sample to the Korean War Project in the hopes that Oliver's remains would someday be identified.

University of Nebraska student Robert Bruce in his 1994 master's thesis on the "Battle of the Chongchon River" said the battle was the worst defeat suffered by the U.S. Army since the fall of Bataan and Corregidor in 1942, claiming more American lives than any other battle ever fought by the U.S. in the post WWII era, namely 1,489 killed.

In September 1976, Teton County veterans placed a plaque in the courthouse naming the county's war dead in the 20th century. Oliver's last name is misspelled as "Field." ▨

Published by the Choteau Acantha September 25, October 9, 16, 2019.

— 24 —
Chicken Raid Turns Deadly
1957

Norwegian immigrant and Power area farmer Toralf Tokerud, 57, was on high alert on March 20, 1957. A number of chickens had been taken from his chicken coop in the few minutes before his discovery, and the culprits appeared to have just driven off.

Carrying his loaded shotgun, Tokerud hopped in his vehicle in pursuit. A short time later he came upon a car that had run out of gas along the state highway. A jury in Teton County District Court, a year after the incident, was asked to determine what happened next in the killing of one Joseph Poitra, 26, on that fateful night.

The Acantha picked up the story on March 28. Tokerud "was released that morning from the Teton County jail when he posted $2,500 bail in the slaying case of Joseph Clifford Poitra, 26, of Hill 57, Great Falls. He is charged with first-degree manslaughter.

"Poitra was fatally wounded late Wednesday night, March 20, near Power following a chicken-stealing escapade at the Tokerud farm. The four companions of the dead man are lodged in the Teton County jail: a cousin, Floyd Poitra, and Marvin Gonzales are charged with conspiracy to commit burglary and Marvin Lapier and Pete Villa are charged with burglary. All the men except Lapier of Browning, live at Hill 57, Great Falls.

"Tokerud's hired man, Gordon Malvin, told the county attorney and sheriff's officers that his employer argued with Poitra, his cousin Floyd Poitra and Gonzales when Tokerud overtook them after their car ran out of gas.

"Malvin said Tokerud ordered the men to roll down their windows and on failing to do so, shot into the car and the blast blew away Joe Poitra's jaw. His cousin Floyd caught a few pellets in his face also.

"Floyd Poitra and Gonzales flagged down a passing motorist who took the wounded man to a Conrad hospital where he died.

"In a statement to the county attorney, Tokerud said he chased Poitra and the three others after he saw them stealing chickens from his place.

"Investigation last Thursday revealed a number of chickens had been taken and several chickens with their necks wrung were found in a borrow pit alongside the highway."

Joe Poitra was born in St. John, North Dakota, near the Turtle Mountain Indian Reservation. He was married and living on Hill 57, the nickname for a neighborhood of "landless" Chippewa-Cree Indians, located three miles northwest of Great Falls. His death certificate lists him as an Indian who died in an "accident." He lived for five hours after entering the hospital, but succumbed from laceration of the brain and massive bleeding. Survived by his wife, 27; a son, 3; and a daughter, 2, Poitra was buried in Mt. Olivet Cemetery in Great Falls.

A year later, the county attorney dismissed the charges against Villa, Gonzales, Lapier and Floyd Poitra.

In March 1958, a jury, after two hours of deliberation, found Tokerud not guilty after a two-day trial before District Judge W.M. Black.

The Acantha stated, "Tokerud, it appeared from testimony at the trial, fired with a shotgun through a window of the Poitra car stalled on the highway near the scene of the chicken-stealing, fatally wounding Poitra, a few shot striking Floyd Poitra who also occupied the car. It is reported that the jury considered it doubtful that Tokerud intended to shoot anyone and that the result of his act may have been accidental."

The jurors were Martin Depner, foreman, Joan Scott, Lester Young, Donald H. Corbett, Arnold Seigle, Louis C. Asmus, Romey McCollom, Francis L. Truchot, Jerry Rapp, LaVerne W. Murr, Nina L. Hilling and Robert L. Broere.

An Acantha story in August 1958 reported that Poitra's wife, Anna Marie, as her late husband's administrator, sued Tokerud for $50,000, but the Cascade County Clerk of Court probate records show no resolution of the wrongful death claim. The story added, "At the trial Tokerud testified his shotgun accidentally discharged when he came up to the car in which Poitra and four companions were seated while he was investigating theft of chickens from his ranch."

Tokerud, 69, a Dutton/Power area resident since 1909, died from cancer in November 1969, in the Teton County Nursing Home and was buried in Dutton Cemetery. ▨

Published in the Choteau Acantha Oct. 31, 2018.

— 25 —
The Canyon Creek Fire
1988

Seeing Haystack Butte totally engulfed in flames is just one of the dramatic events people remember about the Canyon Creek Fire that stormed out of the mountains southwest of Augusta on September 6-7, 1988.

The fire's 19th anniversary passed quietly in 2007, as the normal change to cooler fall weather marked what everyone hoped was the beginning of the end of the annual wildfire season along the Rocky Mountain Front. Then as in 1988, hundreds of firefighters worked fire lines at large wildfires in the mountains west of Choteau as drought-stressed forests of continuous timber burned, periodically filling the air with smoke.

Memories of the 1988 Canyon Creek fire are the stuff of legend in these parts. Augusta area rancher Ray Krone, in a 2007 interview, recalled what happened as if it were yesterday, in a voice tight with anger. He was one of many ranchers who suffered property losses when the fire burned up his fields, haystacks, fences and cattle.

Retired Choteau volunteer firefighters Ben Hoge and James Weinert, and Choteau dozer operator Tom Evensen lived to tell how the wind-driven wildfire overtook their positions as it made a record-setting run almost to Augusta, consuming 160 acres a minute. The men spoke of the fire with awe and with careful words, recalling what went right and what went wrong, as if revealing what they endured might bring down the mythical wind gods, Zephyrus of the west wind and Notos of the south wind, to wreak havoc on the Ahorn and Fool Creek fires burning in the forests west of Augusta and Choteau in September 2007.

Fire strike team leader Craig Cowie of Silver City, N.M., formerly of White Sulphur Springs, was one of 107 firefighters who protected themselves under blanket-like fire shelters during the big blow-up on the night of Sept. 6, 1988. He retold the details of the firestorm event without emotion, reflecting his background as the professional firefighter that he was then and was in 2007, working a two-week rotation as the deputy incident commander for the Ahorn and Fool Creek fires.

Former Great Falls Tribune reporter Ben Lindler and Ron Wakimoto, Ph.D., professor and chair of the Department of Ecosystem and Conservation Sciences, College of Forestry and Conservation in Missoula, provided details of the fire's impact, the former as a professional observer and in 2007 a U.S. Forest Service employee, and the latter as one who was appointed as a technical advisor on the Fire Management Policy Review Team to review what happened during the 1988 fire season in the Greater Yellowstone area. The review included the Canyon Creek Fire in the Bob Marshall Wilderness Complex along the Rocky Mountain Front.

Lightning started the fire on June 25, 1988, in the Canyon Creek drainage of the Scapegoat Wilderness on the west side of the Continental Divide. After hearing favorable long-range weather information, Lolo District Ranger Orville Daniels allowed the fire to burn "by prescription" in accordance with the Scapegoat-Danaher Fire Management Plan of 1982.

The fire remained within the wilderness boundary until Aug. 29, when gusty winds helped increase it to 51,200 acres. The next day the fire burned out of the wilderness boundary, triggering fire suppression efforts. Evacuations began in remote area homes in the Elk Creek area southwest of Augusta and in the Dearborn area, including Diamond Bar X guest ranch.

National Weather Service scientist Dave Goens of Missoula published a technical report in 1990 about "Black Tuesday and Ash Wednesday" (Sept. 6-7). He wrote that the first three of four major wind events to affect the fire were typical for that region at that time of year, but the last one, on Sept. 6-7, occurred under an uncommon and unusual combination of meteorological events. They were "singularly significant and collectively unique," Goens wrote.

People who have lived along the Front all their lives and whose grandparents lived here, have said there was nothing unique about the wind, it was a "Chinook," a dry, warm and steady west and southwest wind that comes and goes regularly.

Regardless, in the end, the livelihoods of scores of Augusta area farmers and ranchers and local outfitters were affected. The Canyon Creek fire burned 247,000 acres, including 40,000 acres of private and state land, 70 million board feet of timber, 200 miles of fencing and six buildings. It killed 200 cows. Ranchers and local firefighters used water pumps to save all the ranch houses in the burn zone, which became islands in a black sea.

"Jim [Weinert] and I spent 17 days on the fire, like a whole lot of other people. You can't predict what Mother Nature will do when she stomps her feet," Hoge said. He was the Teton County Rural Fire Chief at the time of the fire.

In the days leading up to the big blow-up, Hoge attended meetings at the incident command post. He remembered local residents telling the leaders that conditions weren't normal.

"The wind was out of the northeast. It's never like that. 'The wind will switch,' we said, and after eight or nine days, it did. That's when we had the disaster," Hoge said.

According to Goens, the winds were from the east because of a high-pressure zone in eastern Montana and a low-pressure zone in California and Oregon. By Sept. 1, the fire had started to push back on itself on the east side and past control lines on the west and south sides. That lasted for three days, and then on Sept. 4, the weather pattern began to change.

In an interview with Sherry Devlin of the Missoulian newspaper in 2000, Daniels recalled learning of the possibility of the jet stream moving over Montana from the weather service and his reaction. He said he felt helpless hearing the news, but at that point, fire crews could only continue building fire lines as best they could and wait.

By the evening of Sept. 5, Goens writes, a complex pattern of weather events was evolving. A surface wave began to form from a low-pressure center over northern Alberta. It caused low-level southwesterly winds that increased to 34 miles per hour during the night. Then a cool air mass began to override the warm, dry air at the surface.

The westerly surface winds increased during the mid-afternoon as the air masses moved over Idaho and Montana.

That evening the Canyon Creek incident commander ordered firefighters to leave the mountains and at 11 p.m., unburned timber within the fire perimeter ignited because of the hot dry winds and low humidity.

By the morning of Sept. 6, the fire, hotter than normal because of the reburn during the wind reversal, was estimated at 57,000 acres. It had increased by 6,000 acres in five days.

Hoge and Weinert were on the 12-hour nightshift when the winds changed. "We could tell we would have a big problem. You don't have to tell your feet to run. As we were coming down the trail, the fire was spotting ahead of us, a half mile," Weinert said.

Hoge was in charge of assigning firefighters for structure protection of 27 buildings in the Elk Creek drainage.

At 6 p.m. two frontal systems combined with the predicted low-level jet stream. The first front brought 15-mph winds with gusts of 40 mph. At midnight the second air mass moved over the area, and ash began falling in Great Falls, more than 50 miles away. Hoge said the winds sounded like 100 freight trains. For 12 hours, gale-force winds at the mountaintops raced downslope where they intensified, (read complex fluid dynamics here) spreading the flames.

"My objective was to get everybody out," Hoge said, explaining that he and Weinert were the last ones to head down Elk Creek Road. By 10 p.m., the fire was right behind them, the trees were exploding on fire and the mountains on either side were on fire. As they arrived at the fire base camp a few miles outside the forest boundary, they encountered 49 firefighters, (hundreds had already evacuated) sitting in the creek using spray nozzles to rain a protective mist over themselves.

As Hoge stopped his pickup in the open meadow, Fire Safety Officer Ted Twite, a fusee (flare) in his hand, attempted to set a backfire, but it was too late. Running to the county truck, Twite with Weinert pulled out the water hose. Twite sprayed himself and the ground around him, then hosed down Weinert. Hoge, feeling the hot air fill the truck, jumped out and got down on his belly. Twite turned the hose on Hoge and the truck, preventing the fire from igniting their clothes and vehicle as the hot embers flew by and everything burned around them, sparing also the group in the creek.

"Mother Nature did her thing and everybody suffered.

The Forest Service did a tremendous job, but it completely failed. The fire went past the fire lines like they were never there," Hoge said.

Weinert said they left the mountains so fast that they did not start the pumps on John Hoyt's cabin, but the fire surprised them. When they went back up the road a few hours later, Hoyt's cabin was still standing. It hadn't burned, nor did the Elk Creek bottomlands. In fact, the Dearborn River drainage to the south of Elk Creek was spared while the fire consumed the ridges on both sides.

As they went back up the road, Weinert said he called the gal working dispatch in Choteau and told her, "I've been to county fairs, but I've never seen this." He said Haystack Butte was on fire, like a big Christmas tree aglow with 10,000 candles. In another direction, the cottonwood trees around one of the ranchhouses were throwing flames 20 to 30 feet in the air. "It was unreal," he said, and remembered asking himself what he was doing there.

By 6 a.m. the winds had ceased, but beyond the black spikes that were once lodgepole pine and Engelmann spruce, beyond the forest, out on the grasslands, hay bales blazed and mortally wounded cattle that could not outrun the fire or that were stopped by fences, now stood still amid drifts of black ash and wailed, having no hooves to run on, their lower bodies having been consumed by fire.

Hoge and Weinert encountered the cows on the drive out, and reported it via the radio. Deputies authorized to fire a weapon came as quickly as they could to put the cows out of their misery.

The Canyon Creek fire holds the record for the largest single-day fire growth ever recorded. 🔺

Published in the Choteau Acantha Sept. 7, 2007.

2022 Addendum to the Canyon Creek Fire

Driving back to Choteau from Lincoln in late August 1988, Tom Evensen looked west and saw plumes of smoke in the mountains.

A heavy equipment operator at the time, the late Evensen, in a 2007 interview, remembered when a few smoke plumes of the Canyon Creek Fire appeared on the horizon as it burned over the Continental Divide. The sight registered alarm in Evensen and in local residents who made a living along the Rocky Mountain Front.

Tom and his wife, Fava, had lived in Choteau since 1956. He had had plenty of experience fighting fires there, and while working in the North Fork of the Flathead River country, building roads and piling brush with his Caterpillar D7, a medium-sized bulldozer. "Back then, if you had a fire, you would haul the dozer to the fire, load up, and with the men, put it out," Tom said.

Having come from a job building a road at a gold mine in Lincoln, Tom stopped at the Augusta fire camp and inquired whether the firefighters needed any help. "They said no help was needed. They had the fire under control," he remembered, but Evensen had a gut feeling about this one. He left his dozer parked in Augusta — just in case — over by the community church.

"I couldn't believe it. I could see five sets of smoke. On Labor Day, everything changed," Tom said. He and Fava drove to Augusta and got a revised message. "They said, 'Bring everything you've got,'" Tom said.

The invitation would put Tom and George Pearson in the direct line of the Canyon Creek Fire twice over the course of the following few days.

Lightning started the fire on June 25, 1988, in the Canyon Creek drainage of the Scapegoat Wilderness on the west side of the Continental Divide. Based on the National Weather Services's Missoula Fire Weather Unit forecasters' long-range forecast indicating a trend of cooler temperatures with more moisture, which at the time was consistent with the normal August break in the weather in the region, the U.S. Forest Service allowed the fire to burn "by prescription." It remained within the wilderness until Aug. 29, when gusty winds in excess of 30 miles per hour pushed it out of the wilderness boundary, triggering suppression efforts.

On Tuesday, Sept. 6, just as the wildfire started a 16-hour blow up, Evensen loaded his water truck, and his D7 and a Caterpillar D8, a large bulldozer, on lowboys and headed with George Pearson for the Goss ranch in the Smith Creek drainage. At 5 p.m. at the Goss homestead, Tom built a fireguard, a blade-wide band of scraped earth that surrounds a place and stops a ground fire.

That done, the fire boss, who was from Alaska, told Evensen to build a 75- to 80-foot wide fire line, although fire was burning trees on three sides. "It was no use, but that is what he wanted me to do," Evensen said.

At 10 p.m., Evensen went down to the bottom of the Smith Creek drainage because he was hungry, and because, "I wasn't doing any good there. The fire had gone down the draw, and was starting to burn on the other side," he said. Fanned by gusty winds, the Canyon Creek fire was consuming 160 acres a minute.

At midnight a logger went by who had been higher up in the drainage. He stopped long enough to tell Tom, "Get the hell out of here." At the same time, a Forest Service employee came up to Evensen and told him to leave, because they were going to light a backfire. (Note that some of the details about the events over the next two days were confusing in a look back at the 2007 interview and are now lost. Evensen died in 2018 at age 88.)

Pearson was running the D7 and Evensen, the D8. "We were the last two guys there. We loaded the D7 tractor and George drove out with one lowboy and I started to load mine," Tom said. George was a half hour ahead, and to Evensen's amazement, the fire boss had lit a backfire before Evensen had gotten out. "I was surrounded by fire. I took off on a 30-foot-wide gravel road in smoke," he said. In the midst of white, suffocating smoke, he drove alongside running cattle.

The smoke got in the truck and he could not see the roadway. He stopped for a time when he lost all sense of direction. He said he was afraid the heat and fire would melt the tires.

Then the smoke let up momentarily. It was just like driving in a snowstorm, he said. He ran into cows, running like buffalo, and when he finally got over the hill, the air cleared. "I was covered in soot," he said.

Then more smoke, gusts of it, came and he was in a whiteout again. As he went up a hill, it cleared and he saw Charlie Gilsinger's ranch. The man ran out and asked Evensen to build a fireguard. After doing that, Evensen went into Augusta to get something to eat.

By 6 a.m. the fire had concluded its major run. A combination of events, the last being an occurrence of a low-level jet stream that moved over the fire area and remained stationary for 12 hours, put the Canyon Creek Fire into the history books with 240,000 acres burned.

But it was not over for Evensen. In the two days that followed, he got a new assignment to put out spot fires and make fire lines. He and Pearson headed up the Falls Creek drainage to meet a 20-person hotshot crew from Stockton, Calif.

He built a fire line up to the base of Table Mountain and

started plowing a fireguard up to the rock slide there with his D8. He had begun work about 7 a.m. on Sept. 9 and he stopped at noon to eat and look down.

He saw five helicopters using creek water to stop spot fires, but he went back to work with his dozer having been told to pioneer the last 100 yards into a small opening at the base of a scree slope and to construct a safety zone for the crew and the dozer operators to move into.

Tom noted that at about 2 p.m. the smoke was turning black, then white, then brown in color. He made the safety zone about half the size of a football field, then went back up to finish the fire line and finally back down to the safety zone at the edge of the ridge. As the crew and dozer operators assembled in the safety zone, they could see the high winds pushing the flames 30 to 50 feet high in rapid runs below them.

"I was in the cab, when the wind came," he said, describing how, using the dozer, he made a shallow pit and a heat-shield berm piling up dirt four or five feet high. The wind was roaring over the top, and the cat was getting hot, so Evensen tried to make a hole for it to rest in, but he hit solid rock after moving two feet of soil. Evensen sat six feet in the air.

"In walked George who usually worked the morning shift. He wanted to find me and he got there just before the fire blew up, about 3 or 4 p.m.," Tom said.

"We got in the cab and watched the fire coming. I sat in the seat. The wind was so great ahead of the fire, blowing 40 to 50 miles per hour, that embers the size of fingers got into the cab. My Levis were trying to catch on fire so we opened our shelters and looked behind to see the brush outside seared black," he said. The fire was creating its own firestorm.

He remembered the colors, made vivid by sunlight, the

red flames 30 to 35 feet high, then a red brown and then white smoke at the fire moved to grass. An incident report reconstructing the event said that flame lengths in the timber at the top of the ridge as the fire blew out of Falls Creek were around 200 feet.

The heat melted the number "8" made with duct tape on the dozer's window and then cracked it. Looking down through the deck plates, Evensen and Pearson saw black, brown and white smoke as the fire burned the ground under the cab and ran out of fuel.

After a few minutes, the men left the cab, but the smoke was dense. They crawled on the ground and dug holes for their faces and to find better air. The tractor gave the two men shelter, but the investigation that followed reported that nine of the 20 people in the hotshot crew were burned substantially enough to require medical treatment at a Great Falls hospital.

The most damaging intense heat, the report later noted, lasted probably less than a minute. "Several individuals were able to deploy completely but not before receiving some first and second degree burns from radiant heat. A few people, due to wind, heat and malfunctioning seal openers of the plastic inner cases were unable to successfully deploy their shelters and had to double up with others to obtain the needed heat shield protection," the report said. Evensen and Pearson were able to avoid injury.

"There was a movie called 'Red Skies over Montana.' It was like that when we walked out of there. We didn't stop anything. We had a monster on our hands. Even the green trees were skeletons, with no green showing anywhere on the landscape. It was deadly quiet," Tom said.

The crew members, including as many as four women, were in their shelters for about 15 minutes, but then, after waiting more than an hour for the fire runs to subside, they walked to, and washed up at Falls Creek and then out to a bus at the Diamond Bar X Ranch.

Evensen took his dozer down the creek to the Diamond Bar X and then went home. "I'd had enough," he said, noting later that he had lived through an experience of a lifetime.

The next day a critical incident stress team debriefed everyone as part of an investigation. It snowed on Sept. 10-11 and the fires went out. It took an act of nature to start it and one to stop it, Evensen said.

He walked back to the site later and saw that the fire had come to his fire line, but it then jumped a quarter mile.

The incident report found, among other things, that the plan for what the crew and dozers were asked to do on Sept. 9 was inadequate and inaccurate, and that the dozer operators and the hotshot crew were placed in an unnecessary high-risk situation by the tactics assigned. The crew and dozer operators had been placed in a heavy cover of unburned fuels directly in front of the fire's main line of advance, after the division supervisor believed he had a 24-hour delay in the forecasted high winds.

Evensen said one lesson learned was for officials to have more consideration for drought situations. "You've got to look at it knowing that a fire can get away and if it gets too big you can't control it," he said. "I didn't blame anybody. The fire had been at Ovando for weeks," he said. But questions remained as to why the helicopters had not dropped water on the dozers and the hotshots. ▧

— 26 —

Harvest Halted

1989

The extraordinary downpour on Aug. 23, 2014, brought .83 inch of rain that halted harvest, jeopardizing the year's malt barley crop for some farmers. All told, August recorded 1.94 inches of rain where 1.25 inches was normal.

Similarly, the Acantha wrote about almost identical events in August 1989.

"This year's hay and grain crops in this area of Montana are looking very good with reports that the dryland hay crop may be the best ever raised in this area," the Acantha stated on Aug. 3, 1989.

The article continued, "Grain crops are also looking excellent throughout Teton County with farmers holding their breath during the nearly daily thunder and lightning storms which have brought some hail to parts of Montana. With the recent hot weather, grain fields are ripening but harvest is still a-ways off and farmers are getting anxious to get this year's crop in the bin."

On Aug. 17, 1989, the Acantha reported, "Bumper Crop Expected As Harvesting Begins."

Dale Hanson, at that time a manager of the General Mills elevator in Choteau, said farmers had filled their bins, and were bringing their grain to the elevators because they were running out of storage space.

The winter wheat was exceptionally good, said Tim Wilson, Harvest States Cooperative elevator manager.

Hanson said, "The one thing we don't need right now

is rain which could be very damaging to the malting barley crop. It may not hurt the spring wheat too much, but it could be harmful to the winter wheat which is ready to cut."

An Aug. 24, 1989, Acantha photo and caption showed a lineup of trucks delivering grain to the Harvest States elevator the previous Saturday. "Harvest is going well throughout this area, but a hail storm last Tuesday afternoon damaged or wiped out several fields of grain in the Farmington community," went the report. It included the names of eight farmers affected.

The good weather did not last. The Aug. 31, 1989, headline read, "Rains Halt Harvest: Cause Damage to Crops."

"Mother Nature picked an extremely poor time to dump several inches of moisture in Teton County. With harvest in full swing, rains began to fall last Wednesday and continued for three successive days before skies cleared only to cloud up and deposit more rain over the weekend," the article began.

Hanson, Wilson and local Montana State University Extension Agent Bill Richter all agreed that the moisture played havoc with harvest and would cause considerable financial losses to grain growers, especially those raising malting barley which sprouts quickly during wet periods such as was being experienced.

The men worried that many farmers were under contract with Anheuser Busch to sell their barley for $7 per hundredweight, but now might have to sell their product for feed grain for about half that much.

The month of August 1989 turned out to be the second wettest August ever, based on records dating back to 1893. The highest precipitation occurred in August 1933 with a total 4.08 inches, followed by August 1989 with 4.05 inches.

In a September 1989 article Richter offered advice on

the effect of sprouted grain in one's crop, but the unease that prevailed during August waned and an article on Sept. 23, 1989, noted the wheat harvest was unchanged or greater than the previous year, 1988. During that memorable August only .14 inch of rain fell during the entire month, the sixth driest August the county had ever recorded. ▰

Published in the Choteau Acantha September 3, 2014.

Surname Index

www.ingramcontent.com/pod-product-compliance
Lightning Source LLC
Chambersburg PA
CBHW021101090426
42738CB00006B/449